Zen Poetry

Taproot
The Trespasser
Zen: Poems, Prayers, Sermons, Anecdotes, Interviews
Notes for a Guidebook
Heartland: Poets of the Midwest
World of the Buddha: An Introduction to Buddhist Literature
The Pit and Other Poems
Afterimages: Zen Poems of Shinkichi Takahashi
Twelve Death Poems of the Chinese Zen Masters
Zen Poems of China and Japan: The Crane's Bill
Awakening
Heartland II: Poets of the Midwest
Three Zen Poems
Selected Poems
Haiku of the Japanese Masters
The Duckweed Way: Haiku of Issa
The Penguin Book of Zen Poetry
The Duckpond
Prairie Voices: Poets of Illinois
Zen Poems
Encounter with Zen: Writings on Poetry and Zen
Cherries
Bird of Time: Haiku of Basho
Willows
Collected Poems 1953–1983
On Love and Barley: Haiku of Basho
Triumph of the Sparrow: Zen Poems of Shinkichi Takahashi
Bells of Lombardy
Of Pen and Ink and Paper Scraps
The Dumpling Field: Haiku of Issa
The Gift of Great Poetry
Cage of Fireflies: Modern Japanese Haiku
Zen, Poetry, the Art of Lucien Stryk (edited by Susan Porterfield)
The Awakened Self: Encounters with Zen

Zen Poetry
Let the Spring Breeze Enter

Edited and translated by

Lucien Stryk and Takashi Ikemoto

With an Introduction and Afterword by

Lucien Stryk

GROVE PRESS

New York

An earlier, shorter version of this book was published in Great Britain in 1977 by
Swallow Press.

*Published simultaneously in Canada
Printed in the United States of America*

Library of Congress Cataloging-in-Publication Data

Zen poetry: let the spring breeze enter / edited and translated by
 Lucien Stryk, Takashi Ikemoto; with an introduction and afterword
 by Lucien Stryk.
    Rev. and enl. ed. of: The penguin book of Zen poetry. 1977
    ISBN 0-8021-3407-6
    1. Zen poetry—Translations into English. 2. Haiku—Translations
 into English. 3. Japanese poetry—Translations into English.
 4. Chinese poetry—Translations into English. I. Stryk, Lucien.
 II. Ikemoto, Takashi, 1906– . III. Penguin book of Zen poetry.
 PL782.E3Z39   1995   895.6'10080922943—dc20   94-15818

Design by Laura Hammond Hough

Grove Press
841 Broadway
New York, NY 10003

02   10 9 8 7 6 5

To the memory of my cousin Stephen Ullmann
—LUCIEN STRYK

To the memory of my beloved brother Yukio
—TAKASHI IKEMOTO

Acknowledgments

༂⚜༂

Thanks are due to the following for permission to reprint: *American Poetry Review*, *Bleb*, *Chariton Review*, *Chicago Review*, *Harbinger*, *Las Americas Review*, *Loon*, *Mr Cogito*, *Modern Poetry in Translation*, *The Mountain Path*, *New Letters*, *Northwest Review*, Patmos Press (from *the bell of transience*), *Prairie Schooner*, *Rapport*, Rook Press (from *Haiku of the Japanese Masters* and *The Duckweed Way*), Sceptre Press (from *Three Zen Poems*), Swallow Press (from *Selected Poems* by Lucien Stryk), *Thistle*.

Contents

❦

Preface

❧

I

The temple, reached by a narrow mountain path five miles from the bus stop, was in one of the most beautiful districts of Japan. Surrounded by blazing maples, it appeared to have been rooted there for centuries. To its right was a kiln with a batch of fresh-fired pots, to its left a large vegetable garden where a priest bent, giving full attention to a radish patch. He greeted me warmly and at once asked me to stay the night. Talk would wait till evening, after his meeting with parishioners—farmers, woodsmen—to discuss a coming festival. Each, I noticed, brought an offering—fruit, eggs, chestnuts. That time I came with nothing. Twenty years later I brought a book of Zen poems, one of a number I'd translated since that first inspiring meeting.

Poetry had always been part of my life, and my interest in Zen poetry began as the result of that first visit. While teaching in Niigata, I'd been moved by a show of ceramics, calligraphy and haiku poems, and I'd asked a friend to take me to see the artist. The evening of my visit I discovered that the priest's life was devoted equally to parish, ceramics and poetry. He spoke with love of haiku poets—Basho, Issa—and mentioned great Zen masters who excelled in poetry—Dogen, Bunan, Hakuin, names unfamiliar to me.

I was intrigued when he compared their work to certain Western poets (he especially admired a particular passage from Whitman, quoted here near the end of the Introduction), and I resolved to learn something of Zen poetry. He was wonderfully impressive then, and I found him even more so now, this priest-artist content with earth, pots and poems, seeking no praise of the world, his deepest care the people around him. I have owed him all these years a debt of gratitude, both for my feelings about Zen and for the lesson that one should make the most of the earth under one's feet, whether Japan or midland America, which have stemmed in large measure from our meeting.

My second lectureship in Japan, some years after that visit, was in Yamaguchi, the "Kyoto of the West." There, at the Joei Temple, where the great painter Sesshu had served as priest in the fifteenth century, came another meeting which would leave its mark. Takashi Ikemoto, a colleague at the university, and I were interviewing the master of the temple for what later became our first volume of translation from Zen literature. I said things about the rock garden behind the temple—laid down by Sesshu and surely one of the finest in Japan—which struck the master as shallow. He patiently explained that in order to grasp the meaning of so great a work of Zen, I would have to meditate, experience the garden with my being. I was intrigued and humbled. Familiar, through translating the literature, with the ways of Zen masters, I accepted his reproval as challenge. Thus I began a sequence of poems on Sesshu's garden, a discovering of things which made possible not only a leap into a truer poetry of my own but also a more effective rendering of Zen poems.

Years and Zen books since, I still think of those encounters as phases of rebirth. Now, after meetings with Zen masters, poets and artists, comes this volume, the poems translated in homage to those Zenists who insist that awakened life is not a birthright but something to be won through, along a way beyond the self. My experiences, however ordinary and lacking drama they may be, I give here because they are the kind that have always been important to Zen—leading to awareness of possibilities for art and life, which, as the poems reveal, are limitless.

II

Roshi Gempo Nakamura, master of Jishi-in, a sub-temple on the grounds of the important Rinzai temple Nanzenji in Kyoto, is a graduate in Chinese philosophy of Kyoto University. An expert in Chinese literature, especially early Zen poetry, he is a disciple of the late Shibayama Roshi, one of the great modern masters known in the West for his writings and lectures, particularly in the United States, which he visited several times. Shibayama Roshi, who died in 1974, was once master of Jishi-in, and his tomb lies behind the temple. Gempo Nakamura studied with him many years, receiving *inka* (testimony to his enlightenment), one of few so honored by the master, another being Taigan Takayama, a co-translator of *Zen Poems of China and Japan: The Crane's Bill*. Shibayama honored these men, calling them his rarest disciples.

On this brisk October afternoon, the maples on the temple grounds beginning to take on color from the sun, I look forward to my talk with Gempo Nakamura. Master of Jishi-in for thirteen years, since Shibayama Roshi left to serve as chief abbot of Nanzenji, he has tended it well, judging from the garden, one of the most renowned in Kyoto. Rocks placed harmoniously on raked sand, a touch of vivid shrubbery—so beautiful that it's no wonder many come to visit. Such places resemble, in some ways, the colleges of Oxford and Cambridge, a great temple like Nanzenji having a number of small temples circling its main building. The sub-temples use the large refectory and the *Sodo* (meditation hall) in common, each sharing the upkeep of a united whole. From them abbots are chosen to lead the main temple and, as with Nanzenji, its subordinate temples throughout Japan. Rinzai, one of the three chief schools of Zen (the others being Soto and Obaku), has sects, the Nanzenji of Rinzai being one of the most important of these. One day Gempo Nakamura, as his master before him, may be chosen to guide the Nanzenji complex of temples and subordinate temples.

Before our meeting, I wander through Jishi-in with a young disciple studying for the priesthood, who, in turn with fellow disciples, assists the master, greeting visitors and so on. He seems happy to be showing me the temple, which he clearly loves, his home for years to come, while I am awed by the openness of Jishi-in, whose garden can be readily viewed by all. (Most temples these days take entrance fees.) The young disciple has been instructed to take me on to Shibayama Roshi's tomb, for which I am grateful. The dedication in *The Crane's Bill* shows our respect for the late master. His tomb, a simple white stone in the heart of the garden, is destined to be a pilgrims' resting place for Zenists throughout the world. Now I go in to meet Gempo Nakamura, whose welcome is informal in the large reception room overlooking the pattern-sanded garden. Slight, not too carefully shaven, and like all Zen masters disciplined in movement, he begins preparing tea: among many accomplishments, he is an expert in this art. We sip the aromatic tea, speaking casually of common friends. Now, he informs me, he is ready for my questions.

STRYK: As you know, I am interested in the different branches of Zen. Could you give me your idea of the three major sects?

NAKAMURA: The differences, alas, are better known than similarities: Rinzai's insistence on koan interpretation, its often-misunderstood austerities, its indifference to scripture. Yet, like the others, its chief concern is Zen itself. Really a matter of temperament, each offering a unique something to the seeker. The young, feeling need for what Zen offers, can, this day and age, choose, and it's by no means uncommon for students to change sects, in midstream, so to speak. That is, begin with a Rinzai temple or monastery and, for whatever reason, on discovering its ways are not for him (or *her*: you know we have our nuns in Zen), can approach a master of Soto or Obaku, asking to be taught by him. Finding the right master, you see, may be the most important thing of all. Dogen spoke of the danger of dwelling on divisions, maintaining Zen itself the one concern. There—here I am, a Rinzai quoting a Soto master!

STRYK: What is your hope for those who come to train here?

NAKAMURA: That as the result of discipline they are able to live as Zenists—nothing less, or more.

STRYK: What does that mean to a young Japanese?

NAKAMURA: What it has always meant to young Japanese, always. Zen views, after all, are highly distinct.

STRYK: How many working with you are likely to achieve satori?

NAKAMURA: As you've no doubt discovered, there's great reluctance to talk of *that*. What, after all, does it mean?

STRYK: You surprise me. What satori means is surely no secret.

NAKAMURA: Very rarely, however, do we think of it in an absolute sense, and I believe that's what you have in mind. Such awakening is the rarest thing in the world, now as in the past.

STRYK: But the literature is alive with accounts of satori. Surely that's the whole point of discipline. When a master gives *inka,* when you received it from Shibayama Roshi, there's a very definite experience in mind, is there not?

NAKAMURA: Yes and no. You see, one works under a master for years—there are many ways of demonstrating attainment. *Inka* is given only when the master is assured, over a long period, that transformation, sudden or gradual, has occurred. The literature you speak of—and I admit it tends to emphasize awakening—usually concerns a specific event, proper to such literature. But all those things which came before and happen after are, if anything, more important. The daily life of the disciple, the way he conducts himself in and out of the temple, is everything. The master's always sizing up, quite unconsciously: the young man who took you to the *roshi's* tomb, for example, was, I'll confess, observed. Also I wanted to look at *you* before our meeting! In other words, not quite the drama that the literature, especially all those anecdotes about sudden enlightenment, would make it seem. *Inka* is given after many years of close judgment and, yes, friendship. In giving it, the master testifies in no uncertain terms a disciple's training has been satisfactorily completed, that in his judgment he is now able to teach himself. That's almost the prime consideration, for there must be successful transmission if Zen is to be kept alive.

STRYK: Very illuminating, even to one who has lived the literature for years! Attainment, whether leading to a clearly recognized satori or not, is measurable then?

NAKAMURA: Observable may be a better term. All involved in the discipline gain immeasurably, and from the first days of training, it is possible to determine who is likely to succeed. You must understand that only those showing great capacity for sacrifice and hard work are received for training in the first place. This may be during *sesshin,* a few weeks in the coldest and hottest times of year, when those not able to cope with the regimen are noticed and informed that they should not continue. Indeed, only a few expect to give up their conventional life for temple or monastery. Yet things aren't as clear-cut as all that. Often one, unable to cope at first, returns to find he can.

STRYK: And he is permitted to do so?

NAKAMURA: Of course—such people often make the best disciples.

STRYK: Was Shibayama Roshi a strict master?

NAKAMURA: The strictest, and we revered him for that. He encouraged us to think of Zen life as made up of two phases— the attainment of true self, followed by a life of service.

STRYK: Our friend Taigan Takayama would seem to be a good example, wouldn't he? I have in mind the way he serves his community, together with his work as priest. I recall he is director of the council for social welfare of Yamaguchi, as well as that of the prefectural association for the protection of cultural properties. And to top it off, he directs the Yamaguchi orphanage, on the grounds of his temple, Toshunji. I remember how dear he was to those children, a father. Then there is his great interest—one you share, I know—in Zen poetry.

NAKAMURA: Yes, Shibayama Roshi, all of us, were inspired by his dedication. Often Takayama returns for meditation in our *Sodo*. A remarkable man—who does not think himself that at all. Things of little merit, he always says.

STRYK: Is it usual for an enlightened man to come to his home temple for meditation?

NAKAMURA: For meditation, and friendship. Shibayama Roshi encouraged the practice. Without it, one gets caught up in activities, forgetting gradually the primal experience which led to all in the first place. Taigan Takayama believes firmly in the necessity of *zazen*, at which he always excelled.

STRYK: Excelled?

NAKAMURA: Yes. There are differences even when it comes to so basic a part of our life. Takayama sat perfectly while a disciple; everything he did, the humblest task, was performed in the spirit of meditation. He lives as he does today, doing all those things you mentioned, because his meditation was deep and lasting. A true Zenist.

STRYK: Like Takayama, you are interested in the arts, especially Chinese Zen poetry. Could you give me some idea of the way the arts of Japan have been conditioned by Zen?

NAKAMURA: A tall order! Well, I know of your interest in Zen art, and am aware of the way most Westerners associate Zen and art. I would caution against assuming that the connection is absolute. Far from it. There's nothing intrinsically Zen in any art, in spite of the way some seem to reflect Zen principles. It is the man who brings Zen to the art he practices.

STRYK: I see, but surely some arts would not have developed

as they did had it not been for Zen. Haiku, for example. Basho was profoundly Zenist, an enlightened man, and quite possibly for that reason haiku became an important art.

NAKAMURA: There is, to be sure, a strong taste of Zen in his best poems, and it's true he studied Zen with the master Butcho. Perhaps he best illustrates the point I'm making. He brought Zen to the art of haiku, which was well-established before he came onto the scene. It was not really there before him.

STRYK: It might equally be said, would you agree, that there was not true haiku before him? Surely, from Basho on, there's something characteristically Zen-like in the form itself. The greatest haiku contain the sense of revelation we associate with Zen, and there's compression, which resembles that of sumie [ink-wash] painting of artists like Sesshu.

NAKAMURA: Such art is the expression of Zen spirit, whether painting or poetry—and all types of poetry, tanka as well as haiku. Many haiku, those of its finest practitioners, have no Zen whatsoever. No, it is man who fills a poem with Zen. Always man.

STRYK: As that's a problem which most interests me, may we pursue it? I have in mind the various *do* [Ways]—*Kado,* the Way of poetry, for example. As I understand, one follows a particular Way to the heart of Zen. For Eugen Herrigel, it was the Way of archery. Coming to Japan to learn something of Zen, he was informed the best way to grasp it might be through an art, working with a master. It seems he succeeded.

NAKAMURA: I'm familiar with Herrigel's book; it is very convincing, but you must bear in mind he was following his natural bent—since he was deeply interested in the bow. And of course he was fortunate working under one of its greatest masters. I would insist it was he who brought his growing sense of Zen to archery, for there's absolutely nothing in that activity itself which leads to achievement in Zen.

STRYK: Isn't that rather like the old question—Which came first, the egg or the hen?

NAKAMURA: I am being adamant on the point because I feel strongly that Zen is done a disservice by the easy association many make, here as well as in the West, between it and the arts. The problem is more complex than one would suppose. I'm simply maintaining that few works of so-called Zen art, including haiku and *sumie,* have true Zen. It's precisely the feeling that led Professor Awakawa to publish, a few years ago, his remarkable volume *Zenga* [Zen Painting], where he isolates the *sumie* that are true *zenga,* giving reasons, making distinctions. The same might be done with poetry and all other arts. Awakawa quotes, by the way, a fine story concerning one of the Kano School painters who would always tell disciples they must be in a constant state of enlightenment. One day, it appears, while the master lay sick in bed, though it was raining hard, his disciples came to visit. Suddenly the conversation was interrupted by loud singing in the street. "An interesting man," the master said. "Do you understand his state of mind as he walks singing in the downpour? *That's* how you should feel when painting?" The greatest practitioners of the arts we're discussing were profound Zenists—none would deny that. It doesn't follow, however, that when a man lifts brush or pen he is automatically engaging in Zen activity. He may not be the kind to sing in the rain!

STRYK: What, then, if he is in fact a Zenist, meditating, following principles?

NAKAMURA: Wouldn't matter in the least—though perhaps it should.

STRYK: Thus it may be possible for one without knowledge of Zen, even antagonistic to it—I'm being very hypothetical—to produce a true Zen work, something perhaps superior to work of a practicing Zenist.

NAKAMURA: It happens constantly, though I must add at once that, here in Japan at least, there's little of what you call antagonism. We are not a dismissive people, except in politics! Nevertheless, it is certainly possible that one without active interest in Zen might very well produce a superior work.

STRYK: Could it then be truthfully claimed as Zen art?

NAKAMURA: Why? One knows at once whether work has Zen dynamism balanced by composure. One doesn't consult a biography to determine the artist's qualifications. There is *zenki* [Zen spirit] or there isn't, whatever the man calls himself.

STRYK: You put your argument strongly.

NAKAMURA: With good reason. For too many years such associations have been casually made, often by people who should know better. Ours is a distinct Way, its expression in any form unique, rare. Just as attainment is.

STRYK: It must be irksome then to hear people claim to have discovered the truth of Zen?

NAKAMURA: Irksome? Hardly. In any case, I would have to know the people before passing judgments.

STRYK: Does the rebirth, East and West, of Zen give you much satisfaction?

NAKAMURA: As Shibayama Roshi's disciple, how could it fail to? You know how important it was to him.

STRYK: Yet you seem skeptical about the nature of Zen experience?

NAKAMURA: I am a teacher; my life work is to assure the spread of Zen, guiding others to its truth. The claims you speak of do not distress me, so long as those who make them benefit to some degree.

STRYK: That would be enough?

NAKAMURA: Considering what life is for most, more than enough.

STRYK: That makes the master's role very special, doesn't it? Like that of psychoanalyst.

NAKAMURA: No, for we do not treat the ill. Our assumption is not that those coming to us need such attention, but that they seek as conscious beings something beyond self, thus finding the true self. There is an overabundance of analysts in Japan; we do not compete with them. You must bear in mind we accept for training only those who, in our judgment, are clear-visioned, able to train successfully. For the most part, superior persons who might do well at most things.

STRYK: Superior? Surely they must feel some lack to take on a discipline as arduous as Zen.

NAKAMURA: Precisely, because they *are* superior. They feel restless, uncertain, things all feel—but they take action. What they seek, however, is not help with personal problems, of whatever kind, but a Way to truth which makes all such things unimportant. Until they know that Way, they grope in darkness. Yes, what the Zen aspirant seeks is light.

STRYK: And sometimes it flashes suddenly before one?

NAKAMURA: More often it is a small light at the end of a tunnel, approached gradually, becoming larger, brighter, as one nears.

STRYK: To the layman that sounds more like Soto than a Rinzai point of view.

NAKAMURA: Less a lay than Western misconception, I'm afraid. Zen seems so easily understood when such distinctions are made—Soto's gradualness, Rinzai's suddenness, Obaku's middle-of-the-roadness. In reality there are no such distinctions, or at least they are not so profound as some assert. As I've said, there is only Zen and the temperaments of those seeking it. I'm very much afraid most Western books on Zen—many of which, with Shibayama Roshi's help, I've read with care—too often stress dramatic differences. Simple, colorful, but far from truth.

STRYK: That's very humbling, especially to one who writes on Zen! My final question concerns something which interests us both so much, Zen poetry. Would you agree enlightenment and death poems of the masters, Chinese and Japanese, are the most important expressions in the literature of Zen?

NAKAMURA: I would indeed. Especially the death poems, which give the very essence of a life, a brush of wind, and are often pondered like koans by students of Zen. We have always

learnt from them; they are infinitely precious. You are right to be
interested in them.

III

If the mountain priest of Niigata inspired me to feel Zen po-
etry, meeting Master Nakamura, some years later, opened my
eyes to the oneness of Zen and the arts, so that when Takashi
Ikemoto and I moved into this collection we were tracing poets
clearly "singing in the rain." Little is known of the personal lives
of the Chinese masters and laymen herein, other than that they
were Zenists whose path well prepared them for enlightenment.
We chose meditation and death poems from those whose lives
seemed most fully centered in Zen, and who could express them-
selves effortlessly within such brief forms. Each poem was to
become a precious spiritual document destined to be passed on,
generation to generation, to the now.

Records of Japanese masters and haiku poets are, for the
most part, more accurate in time and place. Here again, we sought
out words that touched the heart of Zen and that, of equal impor-
tance, would be seen as poems valuable as works of art. From
Shinkichi Takahashi, considered by many to be the most original
Zen poet of the century, we chose lines most fully expressive of
an extraordinary vision.

When asked in a recent interview, "Could one say that the
more highly charged the 'spiritual energy' of a text—such as one
tends to find in Zen poetry—the more open to interpretive possi-
bility the translator should be?" my response was, "That's exactly
what I have to do as translator . . . rise to the challenge; rise with
passion, even tact, when that is called for. I've never thought of a
translator as someone who should be an apologist, always wor-
ried, hat in hand, about the degree of faithfulness to the original.
But as someone who when working intensely can spark those
magical moments, when in fact he is the equal of the person he is

translating—he must be . . . in order to render the poems properly. This is particularly true of Zen literature: an energy level as great as the poet's, a like degree of linguistic inventiveness, simply has to be there."

Which might suggest that the poems herein, apart from being written by those capable of "singing in the rain," would have to be eminently translatable. Yet I would claim the finest poems, however complex, lend themselves most fully to the voice of their best translator, one who responds to the quality and spirit of the work in hand. Here are pieces taken at random from each of the book's sections, starting with Chinese enlightenment poems:

> *No dust speck anywhere.*
> *What's old? new?*
> *At home on my blue mountain,*
> *I want for nothing.*

This, by Shofu, revealed his awakening, a world surely more tranquil than any he could possibly have imagined when "on the path."

> *Seventy-six; done*
> *With this life—*
> *I've not sought heaven,*
> *Don't fear hell.*
> *I'll lay these bones*
> *Beyond the Triple World,*
> *Unenthralled, unperturbed.*

Fuyo-Dokai, at the age of seventy-six, accepted his fate calmly.

> *Earth, mountains, rivers—hidden in this nothingness.*
> *In this nothingness—earth, mountains, rivers revealed.*
> *Spring flowers, winter snows:*
> *There's no being nor non-being, nor denial itself.*

The Japanese master Saisho, writing this poem as an interpretation of the koan "Joshu's Nothingness," convinced his master that he had won through.

Summer grasses,
all that remains
of soldiers' dreams.

The great haiku poet Basho, who became a monk, affirms in his most revealing work the depth of his awareness.

I'm an unthinking dog,
a good-for-nothing cat,
a fog over gutter,
a blossom-swiping rain.

I close my eyes, breathe—
radioactive air! A billion years
and I'll be shrunk to half,
pollution strikes my marrow.

So what—I'll whoop at what
remains. Yet scant blood left,
reduced to emptiness by nuclear
fission, I'm running very fast.

With "Explosion," Shinkichi Takahashi shows compassionate concern for mankind's fate, in this, our time.

In translating, Takashi Ikemoto and I needed to make poems as impressive as the originals, both within and outside their Zen context, and unless we could do so for these, and all the others, our work would prove meaningless. Yet the translations do possess a quality inherent in all Zen art, whatever the medium, that may be best described as energy coupled with composure. What is most interesting, perhaps, considering the nature of the relationship between master and disciple throughout the fifteen-hundred-year history of Zen, is that in every documented case of a master's judgment concerning the worth of koan interpretations, the poems chosen as most revealing are, by all standards, fine works of art. Take, as an example, these by the Chinese disciple Chokei:

> *Rolling the bamboo blind, I*
> *Look out at the world—what change!*
> *Should someone ask what I've discovered,*
> *I'll smash this whisk against his mouth.*
>
> . . . .
>
> *All's harmony, yet everything is separate.*
> *Once confirmed, mastery is yours.*
> *Long I hovered on the Middle Way,*
> *Today the very ice shoots flame.*

The first piece was rejected as lacking insight by his master, the second joyfully accepted as evidence of the breakthrough. Now, though that was hardly a literary judgment, Chokei's exultation, his newfound energy, convinced his master. I wonder if he also thought it the better poem.

The intention of this book is to reveal, through its poetry, the depth and range of Zen experience. Some might question the inclusion of so many haiku or be puzzled by Shinkichi Takahashi's highly modernist methods. Zen abhors categories, has no interest in conventional structures, whether in poetry or life. When the Zenist chooses poetry as his form of expression, he is conscious only of the need to make his poem revelatory of his experience of the here and now. As a Zenist, he cuts loose from any kind of pigeonholing; he is a "man of no title," who through discipline has made the miraculous return to his "original self."

LUCIEN STRYK

Introduction

✤

I

The Golden Age of China, T'ang through Sung dynasties (A.D. 618–1279), began not long after the Western Roman Empire came to an end and lasted well beyond the First Crusade. One of the most cultivated eras in the history of man, its religious, philosophical and social ground had been prepared centuries before Christianity, and men perfected their lives and arts certain that they gave meaning to something higher than themselves. To artists of the time, numerous and skilled, poetry and painting were Ways—two among many, to be sure, but glorious Ways—to realization of Truth, whose unfolding made possible not only fulfilled life but calm acceptance of its limitations. They saw in the world a process of becoming, yet each of its particulars, at any moment of existence, partook of the absolute. This meant that no distinction was drawn between the details of a landscape—cliffs, slopes, estuaries, waterfalls—shaped by the artist's emotions. Foreground, background, each was part of the process, in poetry as in painting, the spirit discovering itself among the things of this world.

> *On the rocky slope, blossoming*
> *Plums—from where?*
> *Once he saw them, Reiun*
> *Danced all the way to Sandai.*
>
> HOIN

✤

The artist's visions were held to be revelatory; painting, poem meant to put men in touch with the absolute. Judgment of artworks was made principally with that in mind. Some might delight the senses, a few exalt the spirit, whose role was taken for granted to be paramount, the greatest artists respecting its capacity to discover itself anew in their works. Over centuries the West has deduced the guiding aesthetic principle of such art to be "Less is More," and a number of stories bear this out.

One concerns a painting competition in the late T'ang dynasty, a time of many such events and gifted competitors, all of whom, brought up in an intellectual and artistic meritocracy, were aware of what success might mean. Judged by master painters, most carefully arranged, each painting had its theme, that of our story being "Famous Monastery in the Mountains." Ample time was provided for the participants to meditate before taking up brushes. More than a thousand entries of monasteries in sunlight, in shadow, under trees, at mountain-foot, on slopes, at the very peak, by water, among rocks—all seasons. Mountains of many sizes, shapes, richly various as the topography itself. Since the monastery had been described as "famous," monks abounded, working, praying, all ages and conditions. The competition produced works destined to be admired for centuries to come. The winning painting had no monastery at all: a monk paused, reflecting, on a misty mountain bridge. Nothing—everything—more. Evoking atmosphere, the monk knew his monastery hovered in the mist, more beautiful than hand could realize. To define, the artist must have learnt from the Taoism of Lao-tzu or the Zen of Hui-neng, is to limit.

II

Zen began its rapid growth in early T'ang China, a product of the merging of the recently introduced Buddhism of the Indian monk Bodhidharma, who reached China in 520, and Taoism, the reigning philosophy of poets and painters for some thousand years. Providing a rigorously inspiring discipline, insisting on the primacy of meditation, its temples and monasteries were havens for seekers after truth throughout the T'ang, Sung and Mongol-shadowed Yuan dynasties. Zen masters, religious guides, often themselves poets and painters, made judgments concerning the spiritual attainments of artist-disciples on the basis of works produced. Neither before nor since has art had so important a role in community life, and there are countless instances of poems or paintings affecting the development of the philosophy itself. One such concerns the Sixth Patriarch Hui-neng, who was named as Hung-jen's successor chiefly on the strength of his famous enlightenment poem:

The tree of Perfect Wisdom
Was originally no tree,
Nor has the bright mirror
Any frame. Buddha-nature
Forever clear and pure,
Where is there any dust?

Writers of such poems did not think themselves poets. Rather they were gifted men—masters, monks, some laymen—who after momentous experiences found themselves with something to say which only a poem could express. Enlightenment, the point of their meditation, brought about transformation of the spirit; a poem was expected to convey the essential experience and its effect. Such an awakening might take years of unremitting effort; to most it would never come at all:

One day Baso, disciple of Ejo, the Chinese master, was asked by the master why he spent so much time meditating. Baso: "To become a Buddha."

The master lifted a brick and began rubbing it very hard. It was now Baso's turn to ask a question: "Why," he asked, "do you rub that brick?"

"To make a mirror."

"But surely," protested Baso, "no amount of polishing will change a brick into a mirror."

"Just so," the master said. "No amount of cross-legged sitting will make *you* into a Buddha."

Yet masters did their best to guide disciples: one device was the koan (problem for meditation), which they were asked to solve. As no logical solution was possible, the meditator was always at wits' end—the intention. One of the koans, usually first given, was Joshu's "Oak in the courtyard," based on the master's answer to the standard Zen question "What's the meaning of Bodhidharma's coming to China?" These awakening poems, responses to this question of the masters, suggest the range of possibilities:

> *Joshu's "Oak in the courtyard"*—
> *Nobody's grasped its roots.*
> *Turned from sweet plum trees,*
> *They pick sour pears on the hill.*

> EIAN

> *Joshu's "Oak in the courtyard"*
> *Handed down, yet lost in leafy branch*
> *They miss the root. Disciple Kaku shouts*—
> *"Joshu never said a thing!"*

> MONJU-SHINDO

Given their importance, it is not surprising to find in early Chinese enlightenment poems frequent references to koans. Most poems, though, deal with major aims of the philosophy— escape from space-time bondage, for example, a hard-won precondition of awakening:

Twenty years a pilgrim,
Footing east, west.
Back in Suikon,
I've not moved an inch.

SEIKEN-CHIJU

Earth, river, mountain:
Snowflakes melt in air.
How could I have doubted?
Where's north? south? east? west?

DANGAI

Many express swift release from conventional attachments:

Searching Him took
My strength.
One night I bent
My pointing finger—
Never such a moon!

KEPPO

Need for such release, transcending of doctrine (finger pointing at the moon, never taken for the moon itself), was the theme of Bodhidharma's historical interview with Emperor Wu of Liang, shortly after his arrival in China (by then some schools of Buddhism had been established there a few hundred years):

Emperor Wu: From the beginning of my reign, I have built many temples, had numerous sacred books copied and supported all the monks and nuns. What merit have I?

Bodhidharma: None.

Emperor Wu: Why?

Bodhidharma: All these are inferior deeds, showing traces of worldliness, but shadows. A truly meritorious deed is full of wisdom, but mysterious, its real nature beyond grasp of human intelligence—something not found in worldly achievement.

Emperor Wu: What is the first principle of your doctrine?
Bodhidharma: Vast emptiness, nothing holy.
Emperor Wu: Who, then, stands before me?
Bodhidharma: I don't know.

Not long after this Bodhidharma wrote his famous poem:

> *Transmission outside doctrine,*
> *No dependencies on words.*
> *Pointing directly at the mind,*
> *Thus seeing oneself truly,*
> *Attaining Buddhahood.*

As might be expected, awakening poems were held precious in Zen communities, serving for generations as koans themselves or as subjects for *teisho* (sermons). Interpretation was often made in the light of the master's life, what led to his experience. Nan-o-Myo, awakened when asked by his master to interpret "Not falling into the law of causation, yet not ignoring it," wrote:

> *Not falling, not ignoring—*
> *A pair of mandarin ducks*
> *Alighting, bobbing, anywhere.*

Every utterance of a worthy master was thought significant. The late Sung master Tendo-Nyojo, an example, guided Japan's great Dogen (1200–1253) to enlightenment, which alone made his death poem, simple as it is, glorious to the Japanese:

> *Sixty-six years*
> *Piling sins,*
> *I leap into hell—*
> *Above life and death.*

Zen death poems, remarkable in world literature, have a very ancient tradition. On their origin one can only speculate, but probably in early communities masters felt responsibility to disciples beyond the grave, and made such poems in the hope that they would help point the way to attainment, not only for disciples but for posterity. To some the final poem was not felt to be itself of much importance:

> *Life's as we*
> *Find it—death too.*
> *A parting poem?*
> *Why insist?*
>
> DAIE-SOKO

Many, however, considered it to be a symbolic summation, quite possibly preparing well before the inevitable moment. It would stand, every syllable pondered, and lives might well be affected by truth, absolute, whatever its message and worth as "poetry." Differences between death poems give a sense of the variety of temperament among Chinese masters. Fuyo-Dokai's vital self-assurance:

> *Seventy-six: done*
> *With this life—*
> *I've not sought heaven,*
> *Don't fear hell.*
> *I'll lay these bones*
> *Beyond the Triple World,*
> *Unenthralled, unperturbed.*

Koko's sense of release from a harsh existence:

> *The word at last,*
> *No more dependencies:*
> *Cold moon in pond,*
> *Smoke over the ferry.*

Shozan's astringent mockery:

"No mind, no Buddha,"
Disciples prattle.
"Got skin, got marrow."
Well, goodbye to that.
Beyond, peak glows on peak!

There is no way of telling, records being scant and unreliable (there are wild variants of birth and death dates), whether all wrote death poems, but given their solemn purpose they probably did. By 1279, when China was overrun by Mongols, Zen had flourished for almost one hundred years in Japan. There from the start death poems of masters were thought to have great religious meaning. Dogen left, exulting:

Four and fifty years
I've hung the sky with stars.
Now I leap through—
What shattering!

III

Centuries before the introduction of Zen in the Kamakura Period (1192–1333), Japan had been virtually transformed by Chinese Buddhism. Every aspect of life, from the Nara Period (710–84) on, reflected in one way or another the Chinese world vision. Painters and poets looked to China constantly, as did the greatest painter in the Chinese style, Sesshu, who crossed there for instruction and inspiration. Not all became Zenists like Sesshu, who was to join the priesthood, but most were guided by the philosophy, their works revealing the extent. In the earliest Zen communities enlightenment and death poems were written strictly in *kanji* (Chinese characters), in classical verse forms preferred by the Chinese masters—there is little to distinguish poems of the first Japanese Zenists from those written in China centuries before.

Here is the master Daito's enlightenment poem, written when he had succeeded in solving the eighth koan of the Chinese classic Zen text *Hekiganroku,* which contains a reference to "Unmon's barrier":

At last I've broken Unmon's barrier!
There's exit everywhere—east, west; north, south.
In at morning, out at evening; neither host nor guest.

My every step stirs up a little breeze.

And here is Fumon's death poem:

Magnificent! Magnificent!
No one knows the final word.
The ocean bed's aflame,
Out of the void leap wooden lambs.

The Japanese masters composed not only enlightenment and death poems in Chinese verse forms, they often wrote of important events in the history of Zen, like Bodhidharma's interview with the Emperor Wu. Here is Shunoku's poem on the subject. ("Shorin" is the temple where Bodhidharma, on discovering that the emperor lacked insight, sat in Zen for nine years. To reach the temple he had to cross the Yangtze River.)

After the spring song, "Vast emptiness, no holiness,"
Comes the song of snow-wind along the Yangtze River.
Late at night I too play the noteless flute of Shorin,
Piercing the mountains with its sound, the river.

Even in writing on general themes associated with Zen life the masters employed the purest literary Chinese. Since only few Japanese knew the language, this practice made the Zen poems elitist, leading to the feeling on the part of masters like Dogen that an indigenous verse form, tanka (or *waka*), should be utilized.

Such works would be understood in and out of the Zen communities, and surely it was possible to be as inspiring in Japanese, which, though using *kanji*, had a syllabary and was very different from Chinese. The most important collection of early Japanese poetry, the *Manyoshu* (eighth century), contains three kinds of verse forms: *choka*, tanka and *sedoka*, all based on arrangements of 5-7-5 syllable lines, the most popular, tanka, structured as 5-7-5-7-7 syllables—strictly, without any possible variation.

In the Heian Period (794–1185), which immediately preceded the first age of Zen, tanka was the favorite verse form at the courts. Toward the end of Heian, *renga* (linked verse) became popular: a chain of alternating fourteen and twenty-one syllables independently composed but associated with the verses coming before and after. By the fifteenth century, with *renga* expiring of artificiality, something more vital was found—the *haikai renga*, linked verses of seventeen syllables. Later came individual poems of seventeen syllables, haiku, the earliest authentic examples by writers like Sogi (1421–1502), Sokan (1458–1546) and Moritake (1472–1549).

Basho, thought by many Japanese to be their finest haiku writer and greatest poet, lived from 1644 to 1694. Like almost all noted haiku writers he was a Zenist, practicing discipline under the master Butcho, with whom, according to Dr. D. T. Suzuki, he had the following exchange:

BUTCHO: How are you getting along these days?
BASHO: Since the recent rain moss is greener than ever.
BUTCHO: What Buddhism was there before the moss became green?

Resulting in enlightenment and the first of his best-known haiku:

Old pond,
leap-splash—
a frog.

Whether or not they undertook discipline, haiku writers thought themselves living in the spirit of Zen, their truest poems expressing its ideals. To art lovers the appeal of haiku is not un like that of a *sumie* (ink-wash) scroll by Sesshu, and many haiku poets, like Buson, were also outstanding painters.

Zenists have always associated the two arts: "When a feeling reaches its highest pitch," says Dr. Suzuki, Zen's most distinguished historian, "we remain silent; even seventeen syllables may be too many. Japanese artists . . . influenced by the way of Zen tend to use the fewest words or strokes of brush to express their feelings. When they are too fully expressed no room for suggestion is possible, and suggestibility is the secret of the Japanese arts." Like a painting or rock garden, haiku is an object of meditation, drawing back the curtain on essential truth. It shares with other arts qualities belonging to the Zen aesthetic—simplicity, naturalness, directness, profundity—and each poem has its dominant mood: *sabi* (isolation), *wabi* (poverty), *aware* (impermanence) or *yugen* (mystery).

If it is true that the art of poetry consists in saying important things with the fewest possible words, then haiku has a just place in world literature. The limitation of syllables assures terseness and concision, and the range of association in the finest examples is at times astonishing. It has the added advantage of being accessible: a seasonal reference, direct or indirect; the simplest words, chiefly the names of things in dynamic relationships; and familiar themes make it understandable to most, on one level at least. The haiku lives most fully in nature, of great meaning to a people who never feel it to be outside themselves. Man is fulfilled only when unseparated from his surroundings, however hostile they may appear:

> *To the willow—*
> *all hatred, and desire*
> *of your heart.*
> BASHO

White lotus—
the monk
draws back his blade.

BUSON

Under cherry trees
there are
no strangers.

ISSA

In the West, perhaps as a result of fascination with the haiku (its association with the development of modern poetry at one extreme, its universal appeal in schools at the other), it arouses as much suspicion as admiration. It looks so easy, something anyone can do. A most unfortunate view, for haiku is a quintessential form, much like the sonnet in Elizabethan England, being precisely suited to (as it is the product of) Japanese sensibility, conditioned by Zen. For Basho, Buson and Issa, haiku permitted the widest possible field of discovery and experimentation.

The Zen experience is centripetal, the artist's contemplation of subject sometimes referred to as "mind-pointing." The disciple in an early stage of discipline is asked to point the mind at (meditate upon) an object, say a bowl of water. At first he is quite naturally inclined to metaphorize, expand, rise imaginatively from water to lake, sea, clouds, rain. Natural, perhaps, but just the kind of "mentalization" Zen masters caution against. The disciple is instructed to continue until it is possible to remain strictly with the object, penetrating more deeply, no longer looking *at* it but, as the Sixth Patriarch Hui-neng maintained essential, *as* it. Only then will he attain the state of *muga,* so close an identification with object that the unstable mentalizing self disappears. The profoundest haiku give a very strong sense of the process:

Dew of the bramble,
thorns
sharp white.

BUSON

Arid fields,
the only life—
necks of cranes.

SHIKO

To give an idea of the way haiku work, without making an odious cultural comparison, here is Ezra Pound's "In a Station of the Metro," perhaps the most admired (and for good reason) haiku-like poem in English:

The apparition of these faces in the crowd;
Petals on a wet, black bough.

A simile, the poem startles as haiku often do, but much of what is said would, to a haiku poet, be implied. Incorporating the title (haiku are never titled), he might make the poem read:

Faces in the metro—
petals
on a wet black bough.

If asked why, he might answer: the first few words, "The apparition of these," though sonorous enough, add nothing. Nor does the reference to "crowd," metro stations usually being crowded—besides, the "petals" of the simile would make that clear. His revision, he might claim, transforms the piece into an acceptable haiku, one rather like, although perhaps less effective than, Onitsura's:

Autumn wind—
across the fields,
faces.

Without using simile, Onitsura stuns with an immediacy of vision—those faces whipped by a cold wind.

For centuries haiku has been extremely popular, and there are established schools with widely differing views. Typical is the Tenro, truly traditional, working with the 5-7-5 syllabic pattern and a clear seasonal reference, and possessing a creed—*Shasei,* on-the-spot composition, with the subject "traced to its origin." There are around two thousand members all over Japan, and it is usual for groups to meet at a designated spot, often a Zen temple, and write as many as one hundred haiku in a night, perhaps only one of which, after months of selection and revision, will be adequate. It will then be sent to one of the school's masters and considered for the annual anthology, representing poems of some thirty members.

Untypical, by comparison, is the Soun (free-verse) school, which feels no obligation to stick to the seventeen-syllable pattern. Its poems, short and compact, are written in the "spirit of Basho." Their creed is more general—Significance—and is very close to Zen, as many of the members are involved in this discipline. They follow an ancient dictum, *Zenshi ichimi* (Poetry and Zen are one), and *Kado,* the Way of Poetry. As they strive for the revelatory, fewer poems are written than in the Tenro. Both schools, while opposed in principle, relate haiku to Zen, as do all other schools. Yet very few contemporary haiku could have pleased Basho, for however lofty their ideals they are generally derivative.

Kado, the Way of poetry to self-discovery, is similar in aim to other *do* (Ways) of Zen: *Gado* (painting), *Shodo* (calligraphy), *Jindo* (philosophy), *Judo* (force). Haiku teachers and Zen masters expect no miracles of disciples, yet maintain that with serious practice of an art, given aspirations, men perfect themselves: farmers and professors make their haiku, the most egalitarian of arts. To those who find art a mystery engaged in by the chosen, the sight of a haiku-school group circling an autumn bush, lined notebooks and pens in hand, can be sharply touching. Only a cynic would fail to respond.

Only the few, of course, achieve true distinction in the skill and are known to all who care for poetry. Usually they echo early masters, but some find that language cramping and consciously introduce the modern—factories, tractors, automobiles. They will admit, without derogating, to taking little pleasure from old haiku. They are, however, generous readers of one another's work and that of certain contemporary poets. One in whom many are interested, despite his not being a writer of haiku, is Shinkichi Takahashi, who, until his death in 1987, was regarded throughout Japan as the greatest living Zen poet.

IV

On a stone overlooking the sea in a fishing village on Shikoku Island, a poem is carved:

ABSENCE
*Just say, "He's out"—
back in
five billion years!*

It is Shinkichi Takahashi's voice we hear. He was born in 1901, and the commemorative stone, placed by his townsmen, is one of many honors accorded him in recent years; another is the Ministry of Education's prestigious Prize for Art, awarded for *Collected Poems* (1973). In Japan poets are often honored in this way, but rarely one as anarchical as Takahashi. He began as a Dadaist, publishing the novel *Dada* in 1924, and defied convention thereafter. Locked up in his early life a few times for "impulsive actions," when his newly printed *Dadaist Shinkichi's Poetry* was handed to him through the bars of a police cell, he tore it into shreds.

In 1928 Takahashi began serious Zen study under the master Shizan Ashikaga at the Shogenji Rinzai Temple, known for severity of discipline. He trained for seventeen long years, doing *zazen* (formal sitting in meditation) and studying koans—on which he wrote numerous poems. He attained enlightenment (satori) for the first time on reaching the age of forty. In 1953, when fifty-two, he was given *inka* (his awakening testified to) by Shizan, one of seven disciples so honored up to that time. In addition to some fiction and much poetry, he has written books on Zen highly regarded by Zenists, among them *Stray Notes on Zen Study* (1958), *Mumonkan* (1958), *Rinzairoku* (1959) and *A Life of Master Dogen* (1963).

Takahashi has interested fellow-poets and critics, East and West. A Japanese poet writes:

> Takahashi's poetry is piquancy itself, just as Zen, the quintessence of Buddhism, bawls out by means of its concise vocabulary a sort of piquant ontology. . . . Where does this enlivened feature come from? It comes from his strange disposition which enables him to sense the homogeneity of all things, including human beings. It is further due to his own method of versification: he clashes his idea of timelessness against the temporality of all phenomena to cause a fissure, through which he lets us see personally and convincingly the reality of limitless space.

The American poet Jim Harrison comments in the *American Poetry Review* on his "omniscience about the realities that seems to typify genius of the first order," and goes on:

> Nothing is denied entrance into these poems. . . . All things are in their minutely suggestive proportions, and given an energy we aren't familiar with. . . . Part of the power must come from the fact that the poet has ten thousand centers as a Zenist, thus is virtually centerless.

Philosophical insight is uncommon enough, but its authentic expression in poetry is extremely rare, whether found in T. S. Eliot's "Four Quartets" or in Shinkichi Takahashi's "Shell":

Nothing, nothing at all
is born,
dies, the shell says again
and again
from the depth of hollowness.
Its body
swept off by tide—so what?
It sleeps
in sand, drying in sunlight,
bathing
in moonlight. Nothing to do
with sea
or anything else. Over
and over
it vanishes with the wave.

On one level this is a "survivor" poem, inspiring in its moral grandeur; on another, surely important to the poet, it expresses dramatically Zen's unfathomable emptiness. Here is the Chinese master Tao-hsin, Zen's Fourth Patriarch, in a sermon on "Abandoning the Body":

> The method of abandoning the body consists first in meditating on Emptiness. . . . Let the mind together with its world be quietened down to a perfect state of tranquillity; let thought be cast in the mystery of quietude, so that the mind is kept from wandering from one thing to another. When the mind is tranquillized in its deepest abode, its entanglements are cut asunder . . . the mind in its absolute purity is the void itself. How almost unconcerned it appears. . . . Emptiness, non-striving, desirelessness, formlessness— this is true emancipation.

According to the great Taoist philosopher Chuang-tzu, his admirer, Tao-hsin said, "Heaven and earth are one finger." In the poem "Hand," Takahashi writes, "Snap my fingers—/ time's no more." He concludes, "My hand's the universe, / it can do anything." While such a poem may show indebtedness to masters like Tao-hsin, in a piece like the following, deceptively light, the poet's grasp is equally apparent:

AFTERNOON

My hair's falling fast—
this afternoon
I'm off to Asia Minor.

Always in Takahashi there is evidence of profound Zen, in itself distinguishing. His appeal, though, is by no means limited to Zenists, for his imagination has dizzying power: cosmic, surging through space and time ("Atom of thought, ten billion years—/ one breath, past, present, future"), it pulls one beyond reality. At times, among his sparrows, he resembles the T'ang master Niaok'e (Bird's Nest), so called because he meditated high in a tree, wise among the creatures.

Yet Takahashi is never out of this world, which for Zenists is a network of particulars, each reflecting the universal and taking reality from its relationship to all others: it has otherwise no existence. This doctrine of Interpenetration, as known in Zen and all other schools of Mahayana Buddhism, cannot be understood without being felt: to those incapable of feeling, such ideals have been thought mere "mysticism." Poets and philosophers have attempted for centuries to explain interdependence. Here is the late second-century Indian philosopher Pingalaka:

> If the cloth had its own fixed, unchangeable self-essence, it could not be made from the thread . . . the cloth comes from the thread and the thread from the flax. . . . It is just like the . . . burning and the burned. They are brought together under certain conditions, and thus there takes place a phenomenon called burning . . . each has no reality of its own. For when one is absent the other is put out of existence. It is so with all things in this world, they are all empty, without self, without absolute existence. They are like the will-o'-the-wisp.

For one who believes in the interpenetration of all living things, the world is a body, and if he is a poet like Takahashi, troubled by what the unenlightened inflict upon one another, he will write:

Why this confusion,
how restore the ravaged
body of the world?

And against this confusion he will invoke the saving force of Buddhism, the layman Vimalakirti who "at a word draws galaxies to the foot of his bed," and Buddha himself, in a poem like "Spinning Dharma Wheel," which ends:

Three thousand years since Buddha
found the morning star—now
sun itself is blinded by his light.

The poet once wrote, "We must model ourselves on Bodhidharma, who kept sitting till his buttocks grew rotten. We must have done with all words and letters, and attain truth itself." This echo of Lao-tzu in the Taoist classic *Tao Teh Ching* ("He who knows does not speak") is, as truth, relative: to communicate his wisdom, Lao-tzu had to speak, and Takahashi's voice is inexhaustible. No one would question his seriousness, the near doctrinal tone of some of his work, yet his best poems pulse with *zenki* (Zen dynamism), flowing spontaneously from the formless self and partaking of the world's fullness:

CAMEL
The camel's humps
shifted with clouds.

Such solitude beheads!
My arms stretch

beyond mountain peaks,
flame in the desert.

xlv

V

Such are the three major phases of Zen poetry, spanning nearly 1,500 years from the earliest examples to the present, and displaying distinctive characteristics: the Chinese master Reito would very likely have appreciated Shinkichi Takahashi, much as Takahashi values Reito. This consistency, while very special, is by no means inexplicable. The philosophy underlying the poetry is today, in every respect, precisely what it was in T'ang China: it worked then, it works now, in the face of all that would seem bent on undermining it. In Japan, where industry is king, the need for Zen intensifies, and particular care is taken to preserve its temples and art treasures, numbered among the nation's glories.

Perhaps today Zen's spirit shines most purely in its poetry, some of which is familiar to all, wherever they happen to live and however limited their knowledge of the philosophy. Yet consciously or not, those who care for Fuyo-Dokai, Issa or Shinkichi Takahashi *know* Zen—as much as those who revere Mu-ch'i and Sesshu. For to respond strongly to poetry and painting is to understand the source of their inspiration, just as to relate fully to others is to understand Zen's interpenetration—more completely than do those who, though familiar with its terminology, are incapable of attaining its spiritual riches. Walt Whitman, a poet much admired by Zenists, wrote in "Song for Occupations":

> *We consider bibles and religions divine—I do not say*
> *they are not divine,*
> *I say they have all grown out of you, and may grow out*
> *of you still,*
> *It is not they who give the life, it is you who give the life,*
> *Leaves are not more shed from the trees, or trees from*
> *the earth, than they are shed out of you.*

Zen always traveled well in time and space, through denying them. Its poetry will continue to move some to heroic efforts toward light, constantly delight others—which is as it should be. "Zen is offering something," the master Taigan Takayama said, "and offering it directly. People just can't seem to grasp it." Zen not only offers itself directly, but everywhere, and nowhere more authentically than in poems written in its name and honor, as the Chinese layman Sotoba realized nearly a thousand years ago when he wrote in his enlightenment:

> *The mountain—Buddha's body.*
> *The torrent—his preaching.*
> *Last night, eighty-four thousand poems.*
> *How, how make them understand?*

LUCIEN STRYK

A Note on the Translation

꙳

In 1972, in my Introduction to the most recent of our co-translations of Zen poetry, I wrote: "It is high time for Western intellectuals to turn more attention than ever to the appreciation of Zen poetry." Since then the situation appears to have improved somewhat, as attested by a continuing demand for the collections of Zen poems in our rendering—above all, for Shinkichi Takahashi's poems. Heartened by our readers' favorable response, we set about preparing another co-translation two years ago, but my illness, critical at one time, prevented fruition of the project. Luckily enough, however, and thanks ultimately to Zen vitality in myself, this crisis has passed and we have finally succeeded in producing this book for the Western reader.

Our translation, I acknowledge, is often free, occasionally to such a degree that the reader, if he has a familiarity with the original language, may judge a good number of the pieces to be adaptations rather than translations. This may especially be felt with Takahashi. His original verse is sometimes pithy, at other times lengthy and, one might almost say, prosaic. In the former case our rendering is verbally faithful to the originals; in the latter, some part is omitted, with the result that a number of the originals are turned into compact vignettes. This is the outcome of our policy on verse translation: translation is re-creation; and it is realized through Lucien Stryk's poetic intuition and linguistic skill. Our co-translation is finally Stryk's translation, as will be evident to the discerning eye of Western readers of poetry. Which leads me to say a few words on one aspect of the translation of Japanese/Chinese Zen poetry.

At present there can be few, if any, Japanese or Westerners capable of carrying out single-handedly this particular literary work. The requirements are clear: a would-be translator must possess rich practical experience of orthodox Zen, an ability to write English poetry and a thorough knowledge of Japanese/Chinese literature. To satisfy just one of these requirements demands many years, or indeed a lifetime, of training. That is why, as a second best, I have adopted the joint-translation method and, most fortunately, I have found in Lucien Stryk an unsurpassable collaborator. In the United States he is often described as a Zen poet, which appellation he fully deserves. It is not that he has subjected himself to regular discipline (Zen-sitting, etc.) in a Zen temple; rather, just as D. T. Suzuki once declared that his friend Kitaro Nishida, the noted Zen philosopher, had identified himself with Zen truth via sheer philosophical speculation, so Stryk has gained a high degree of Zen-identification by means of his poetical experience. Thus my own principal contribution to this joint translation is to supply Stryk with more or less literal translations and to examine his versions of the poems.

I have already touched upon Stryk's treatment of Takahashi's work: the concise, pithy rendering, whether of short or long pieces. His poetical genius is in its own way sufficiently flexible to adapt itself to any form of verse. Even so, he often seems to be particularly drawn to the shorter pieces, and it is therefore appropriate that he has recently come to be attracted by haiku, and proposed to me that we devote a section of this book to them. In my opinion the haiku included here eminently satisfy a vital criterion of all good translations—that they possess a vigorous life of their own. The reader may find it interesting to compare the following versions, by nine different translators, of a haiku by Basho (N.B. numbers 3 and 6 are by Japanese translators; Stryk's is number 9):

1   Ta'en ill while journeying, I dreamt
      I wandered o'er withered moor.

2   At midway of my journey fallen ill,
       To-night I fare again,
      In dream, across a desert plain.

3   Lying ill on journey
      Ah, my dreams
      Run about the ruin of fields.

4   Nearing my journey's end,
      In dreams I trudge the wild waste moor,
      And seek a kindly friend.

5   On a journey ta'en ill—
      My dream a dried-up plain,
      Through which I wander.

6   Taken ill on my travels,
      My dreams roam over withered moors.

7   On a journey, ill—
      and my dreams, on withered fields
      are wandering still.

8   Ailing on my travels,
      Yet my dream wandering
      Over withered moors.

9   Sick on a journey—
      over parched fields
      dreams wander on.

There are several ways of reading Zen verse; for instance, the reader may approach it with satori as an object, or for critical appreciation, or simply for pleasure. In this respect, one probably should not be too rigorous; Zen verse should be accessible to all sorts of readers. But it appears to me that the days may not be very distant when English-speaking readers will find in Zen poetry a source of pure pleasure. I hope that this book will contribute to the creation of such an atmosphere.

In concluding this Note, my hearty thanks are due to the following:

Master Taigan Takayama of Yamaguchi and Master Gempo Nakamura of Kyoto, learned young disciples of the late Abbot Zenkei Shibayama of Nanzenji Temple, Kyoto; the former furnished me with the Japanese-style readings of the Chinese Zenists' originals, frequently accompanying them with brief comments, while the latter enlightened me as to my questions about interpretation of some Chinese pieces. The Zen poet Shinkichi Takahashi, though he happened to be taking a complete rest, clarified for me a term in one of his poems.

The friendly cooperation of the above Zenists has richly contributed to securing for our book precision—not formal but essential—which, I hope, will be counted among its features.

TAKASHI IKEMOTO
In a suburb of Kyoto, Japan
November 1976

Zen Poetry

If you study Japanese art, you see a man who is undoubtedly wise,
philosophic and intelligent, who spends his time how? In study-
ing the distance between the earth and the moon? No. In study-
ing the policy of Bismarck? No. He studies a single blade of grass.
But this blade of grass leads him to draw every plant and then the
seasons, the wide aspects of the countryside, then animals, then
the human figure. So he passes his life, and life is too short to do
the whole.

VINCENT VAN GOGH TO HIS BROTHER THEO, ARLES, 1888

Who dares approach the lion's
Mountain cave? Cold, robust,
A Zen-man through and through,
I let the spring breeze enter at the gate.

DAIGU (1584–1669)

Part One

Chinese Poems of
Enlightenment and Death

NOTE: Most of the following Chinese masters and laymen, sixty in all, flourished during the Southern Sung dynasty (1127–1279), but their exact dates, with some exceptions, are missing in biographical records of Chinese Zenists. Among those who can be dated, Mumon-Ekai (Rinzai sectarian and author of *Mumonkan: The Gateless Barrier,* one of the most celebrated collections of disciplinary Zen questions and answers), Tendo-Nyojo (instructor in Soto Zen of Dogen, who, returning home from the Continent, founded the Japanese Soto sect) and Daie-Soko (Rinzai Zen leader with a large following) stand out as brilliant figures in Chinese Zen history.

Enlightenment

꧁

Ox bridle tossed, vows taken,
I'm robed and shaven clean.
You ask why Bodhidharma came east—
Staff thrust out, I hum like mad.

REITO

Twenty years a pilgrim,
Footing east, west.
Back in Seiken,
I've not moved an inch.

SEIKEN-CHIJU

Once the goal's reached,
Have a good laugh.
Shaven, you're handsomer—
Those useless eyebrows!

KISHU

The old master held up fluff
And blew from his palm,
Revealing the Source itself.
Look where clouds hide the peak.

KAIGEN

꧁

The mountain—Buddha's body.
The torrent—his preaching.
Last night, eighty-four thousand poems.
How, how make them understand?

LAYMAN SOTOBA (1036–1101)

How long the tree's been barren.
At its tip long ropes of cloud.
Since I smashed the mud-bull's horns,
The stream's flowed backwards.

HOGE

Joshu's "Oak in the courtyard"—
Nobody's grasped its roots.
Turned from sweet plum trees,
They pick sour pears on the hill.

EIAN

On the rocky slope, blossoming
Plums—from where?
Once he saw them, Reiun
Danced all the way to Sandai.

HOIN

Joshu's "Oak in the courtyard"
Handed down, yet lost in leafy branch
They miss the root. Disciple Kaku shouts—
"Joshu never said a thing!"

MONJU-SHINDO

No dust speck anywhere.
What's old? new?
At home on my blue mountain,
I want for nothing.

SHOFU

Over the peak spreading clouds,
At its source the river's cold.
If you would see,
Climb the mountain top.

HAKUYO

Loving old priceless things,
I've scorned those seeking
Truth outside themselves:
Here, on the tip of the nose.

LAYMAN MAKUSHO

Traceless, no more need to hide.
Now the old mirror
Reflects everything—autumn light
Moistened by faint mist.

SUIAN

No mind, no Buddhas, no live beings,
Blue peaks ring Five Phoenix Tower.
In late spring light I throw this body
Off—fox leaps into the lion's den.

CHIFU

Sailing on Men River, I heard
A call: how deep, how ordinary.
Seeking what I'd lost,
I found a host of saints.

SOAN

In serving, serve,
In fighting, kill.
Tokusan, Ganto—
A million-mile bar!

JINZU

Years keeping *that* in mind,
Vainly questioning masters.
A herald cries, "He's coming!"
Liver, gall burst wide.

ANBUN

Seamless—
Touched, it glitters.
Why spread *such* nets
For sparrows?

GOJUSAN

Clear, clear—clearest!
I ran barefoot east and west.
Now more lucid than the moon,
The eighty-four thousand
Dharma gates!

MOAN

I set down the emerald lamp,
Take it up—exhaustless.
Once lit,
A sister is a sister.

GEKKUTSU-SEI

Not falling, not ignoring—
A pair of mandarin ducks
Alighting, bobbing, anywhere.

NAN-O-MYO

How vast karma,
Yet what's there
To cling to? Last night,
Turning, I was blinded
By a ray of light.

SEIGEN-YUIIN

A deafening peal,
A thief escaped
My body. What
Have I learnt?
The Lord of Nothingness
Has a dark face.

LAYMAN YAKUSAI

A thunderbolt—eyes wide,
All living things bend low.
Mount Sumeru dances
All the way to Sandai.

MUMON-EKAI (1183–1260)

Where is the dragon's cave?
Dozing this morn in Lord Sunyata's
Palace, I heard the warbler.
Spring breeze shakes loose
The blossoms of the peach.

KANZAN-SHIGYO

No mind, no Buddha, no being.
Bones of the Void are scattered.
Why should the golden lion
Seek out the fox's lair?

TEKKAN

Earth, river, mountain:
Snowflakes melt in air.
How could I have doubted?
Where's north? south? east? west?

DANGAI

Joshu's word—Nothingness.
In spring blossom everywhere.
Now insight's mine,
Another dust-speck in the eye!

KUCHU

Joshu exclaimed, "Dog's no Buddha,"
All things beg for life.
Even the half-dead snake
Stuffed in the basket.
Giving to haves, taking from
Have-nots—never enough.

ICHIGEN

Searching Him took
My strength.
One night I bent
My pointing finger—
Never such a moon!

KEPPO

Death

The fiery unicorn snapped
Its golden chain, moon-hare
Flung wide the silver gate:
Welcome, over Mount Shozan,
The midnight moon.

DAICHU

Seventy-six: done
With this life—
I've not sought heaven,
Don't fear hell.
I'll lay these bones
Beyond the Triple World,
Unenthralled, unperturbed.

FUYO-DOKAI (1042–1117)

A rootless tree,
Yellow leaves scattering
Beyond the blue—
Cloudless, stainless.

SOZAN-KYONIN (9th century?)

Sixty-five years,
Fifty-seven a monk.
Disciples, why ask
Where I'm going,
Nostrils to earth?

UNPO BUN-ETSU

The word at last,
No more dependencies:
Cold moon in pond,
Smoke over the ferry.

KOKO

Sixty-six years
Piling sins,
I leap into hell—
Above life and death.

TENDO-NYOJO (1163–1228)

Sky's not high, earth not solid—
Try to see! Look,
This day, December 25th,
The Northern Dipper blazes south.

SEIHO

Way's not for the blind:
Groping, they might as well
Seek in the Dipper.
Old for Zen combat, only
The plough will comprehend:
I'll climb Mount Kongo, a pine.

TOZAN-GYOSO

"No mind, no Buddha,"
Disciples prattle.
"Got skin, got marrow."
Well, goodbye to that.
Beyond, peak glows on peak!

SHOZAN

Nothing longed for,
Nothing cast off.
In the great Void—
A, B, C, D.
One blunder, another,
Everyone seeking
Western Paradise!

LAYMAN YOKETSU

Wino, always stumbling,
Yet in drinking
I show most discretion.
Where to wind up,
Sober, this evening?
Somewhere on the river bank
I'll find dawn's moon.

HOMYO

Sky-piercing sword, gleaming cold,
Cuts Demons, Buddhas, Patriarchs,
Then moonlit, stirred by wind, sinks
In its jeweled scabbard. Iron bulls
Along the river bank plunge everywhere.

ZUIAN

Talking: seven steps, eight falls.
Silent: tripping once, twice.
Zenists everywhere,
Sit, let the mind be.

SHISHIN-GOSHIN (?–1339)

High wind, cold moon,
Long stream through the sky.
Beyond the gate, no shadow—
Four sides, eight directions.

SHOKAKU

Today Rakan, riding an iron horse
Backwards, climbs Mount Sumeru.
Galloping through Void,
I'll leave no trace.

RAKAN-KEINAN

This fellow, perfect in men's eyes,
Utters the same thing over
And over, fifty-six years. Now
Something new—spear trees, sword hills!

IKUO-JOUN

No more head shaving,
Washing flesh.
Pile high the wood,
Set it aflame!

CHITSU

Forty-nine years—
What a din!
Eighty-seven springs—
What pleasures!
What's having? not having?
Dreaming, dreaming.
Plum trees snow-laden,
I'm ready!

UNCHO

Life's as we
Find it—death too.
A parting poem?
Why insist?

DAIE-SOKO (1089–1163)

Iron tree blooms,
Cock lays an egg.
Over seventy, I cut
The palanquin ropes.

WAKUAN-SHITAI (1108–69)

Seventy-two years I've hung
The karma mirror.
Smashing through,
I'm on the Path!

IKUO-MYOTAN

All things come apart.
No saintly sign
In these poor bones—
Strew their ashes
Onto Yangtze waves.
The First Principle, everywhere.

DAISEN

Eighty-three years—at last
No longer muzzled.
The oak's a Buddha,
Void's pulled down.

KYURIN-EKI

Finally out of reach—
No bondage, no dependency.
How calm the ocean,
Towering the Void.

TESSHO

Fifty-three years
This clumsy ox has managed,
Now barefoot stalks
The Void—what nonsense!

SEKISHITSU-SOEI

Coming, I clench my hands,
Going, spread them wide.
Once through the barrier,
A lotus stem will
Drag an elephant!

DANKYO-MYORIN (13th century)

Seventy-eight awkward years—
A clownish lot. The mud-bull
Trots the ocean floor.
In June, snowflakes.

ICHIGEN

How Zenists carry on
About the birthless!
What madness makes me toll,
At noon, the midnight bell?

GEKKO-SOJO

This body won't pollute
The flowering slope—
Don't turn that earth.
What need a *samadhi* flame?
Heaped firewood's good enough.

SEKIOKU-SEIKYO

Mount Sumeru—my fist!
Ocean—my mouth!
Mountain crumbles, ocean dries.
Where does the jeweled hare leap,
Where reels the golden crow?

KIKO

Part Two

Poems of the Japanese
Zen Masters

The Western Patriarch's doctrine is transplanted!
I fish by moonlight, till on cloudy days.
Clean, clean! Not a worldly mote falls with the snow
As, cross-legged in this mountain hut, I sit the evening through.

DOGEN (1200–1253)

Coming, going, the waterfowl
Leaves not a trace,
Nor does it need a guide.

DOGEN

The all-meaning circle:
No in, no out;
No light, no shade.
Here all saints are born.

SHOICHI (1202–80)

Clear in the blue, the moon!
Icy water to the horizon,
Defining high, low. Startled,
The dragon uncoils about the billows.

RYUZAN (1274–1358)

Invaluable is the Soto Way—
Why be discipline's slave?
Snapping the golden chain,
Step boldly towards the sunset!

GASAN (1275–1365)

Many times the mountains have turned from green to yellow—
So much for the capricious earth!
Dust in your eyes, the triple world is narrow;
Nothing on the mind, your chair is wide enough.

MUSO (1275–1351)

Vainly I dug for a perfect sky,
Piling a barrier all around.
Then one black night, lifting a heavy
Tile, I crushed the skeletal void!

MUSO

At last I've broken Unmon's barrier!
There's exit everywhere—east, west; north, south.
In at morning, out at evening; neither host nor guest.
My every step stirs up a little breeze.

DAITO (1282–1337)

To slice through Buddhas, Patriarchs
I grip my polished sword.
One glance at my mastery,
The void bites its tusks!

DAITO

I moved across the Dharma-nature,
The earth was buoyant, marvelous.
That very night, whipping its iron horse,
The void galloped into Cloud Street.

GETSUDO (1285–1361)

Thoughts arise endlessly,
There's a span to every life.
One hundred years, thirty-six thousand days:
The spring through, the butterfly dreams.

DAICHI (1290–1366)

Refreshing, the wind against the waterfall
As the moon hangs, a lantern, on the peak
And the bamboo window glows. In old age mountains
Are more beautiful than ever. My resolve:
That these bones be purified by rocks.

JAKUSHITSU (1290–1367)

He's part of all, yet all's transcended;
Solely for convenience he's known as master.
Who dares say he's found him?
In this rackety town I train disciples.

CHIKUSEN (1292–1348)

All night long I think of life's labyrinth—
Impossible to visit the tenants of Hades.
The authoritarian attempt to palm a horse off as deer
Was laughable. As was the thrust at
The charmed life of the dragon. Contemptible!
It's in the dark that eyes probe earth and heaven,
In dream that the tormented seek present, past.
Enough! The mountain moon fills the window.
The lonely fall through, the garden rang with cricket song.

BETSUGEN (1294–1364)

Beyond the snatch of time, my daily life.
I scorn the State, unhitch the universe.
Denying cause and effect, like the noon sky,
My up-down career: Buddhas nor Patriarchs can convey it.

JUO (1296–1380)

Magnificent! Magnificent!
No one knows the final word.
The ocean bed's aflame,
Out of the void leap wooden lambs.

FUMON (1302–69)

For all these years, my certain Zen:
Neither I nor the world exist.
The sutras neat within the box,
My cane hooked upon the wall,
I lie at peace in moonlight
Or, hearing water plashing on the rock,
Sit up: none can purchase pleasure such as this:
Spangled across the step-moss, a million coins!

SHUTAKU (1308–88)

Mind set free in the Dharma-realm,
I sit at the moon-filled window
Watching the mountains with my ears,
Hearing the stream with open eyes.
Each molecule preaches perfect law,
Each moment chants true sutra:
The most fleeting thought is timeless,
A single hair's enough to stir the sea.

SHUTAKU

Why bother with the world?
Let others go gray, bustling east, west.
In this mountain temple, lying half-in,
Half-out, I'm removed from joy and sorrow.

RYUSHU (1308–88)

After the spring song, "Vast emptiness, no holiness,"
Comes the song of snow-wind along the Yangtze River.
Late at night I too play the noteless flute of Shorin,
Piercing the mountains with its sound, the river.

SHUNOKU (1311–88)

How heal the phantom body of its phantom ill,
Which started in the womb?
Unless you pluck a medicine from the Bodhi-tree,
The sense of karma will destroy you.

TESSHU (14th century)

Not a mote in the light above,
Soul itself cannot offer such a view.
Though dawn's not come, the cock is calling:
The phoenix, flower in beak, welcomes spring.

TSUGEN (1322–91)

Men without rank, excrement spatulas,
Come together, perfuming earth and heaven.
How well they get along in temple calm
As, minds empty, they reach for light.

GUCHU (1323–1409)

Life: a cloud crossing the peak.
Death: the moon sailing.
Oh just once admit the truth
Of noumenon, phenomenon,
And you're a donkey-tying pole!

MUMON (1323–90)

Inscription over His Door
He who holds that nothingness
Is formless, flowers are visions,
Let him enter boldly!

GIDO (1325–88)

Riding backwards this wooden horse,
I'm about to gallop through the void.
Would you seek to trace me?
Ha! Try catching the tempest in a net.

KUKOKU (1328–1407)

The void has collapsed upon the earth,
Stars, burning, shoot across Iron Mountain.
Turning a somersault, I brush past.

ZEKKAI (1336–1405)

The myriad differences resolved by sitting, all doors opened.
In this still place I follow my nature, be what it may.
From the one hundred flowers I wander freely,
The soaring cliff—my hall of meditation
(With the moon emerged, my mind is motionless).
Sitting on this frosty seat, no further dream of fame.
The forest, the mountain follow their ancient ways,
And through the long spring day, not even the shadow of a bird.

REIZAN (?–1411)

Defying the power of speech, the Law Commission on Mount
    Vulture!
Kasyapa's smile told the beyond-telling.
What's there to reveal in that perfect all-suchness?
Look up! the moon-mind glows unsmirched.

MYOYU (1333–93)

My eyes eavesdrop on their lashes!
I'm finished with the ordinary!
What use has halter, bridle
To one who's shaken off contrivance?

EICHU (1340–1416)

Last year in a lovely temple in Hirosawa,
This year among the rocks of Nikko,
All's the same to me:
Clapping hands, the peaks roar at the blue!

HAKUGAI (1343–1414)

Splitting the void in half,
Making smithereens of earth,
I watch inching towards
The river, the cloud-drawn moon.

NANEI (1363–1438)

Serving the Shogun in the capital,
Stained by worldly dust, I found no peace.
Now, straw hat pulled down, I follow the river:
How fresh the sight of gulls across the sand!

KODO (1370–1433)

For seventy-two years
I've kept the ox well under.
Today, the plum in bloom again,
I let him wander in the snow.

BOKUO (1384–1455)

After ten years in the red-light district,
How solitary a spell in the mountains.
I can see clouds a thousand miles away,
Hear ancient music in the pines.

IKKYU (1394–1481)

Void in Form

When, just as they are,
White dewdrops gather
On scarlet maple leaves,
Regard the scarlet beads!

IKKYU

Form in Void

The tree is stripped,
All color, fragrance gone,
Yet already on the bough,
Uncaring spring!

IKKYU

Taking hold, one's astray in nothingness;
Letting go, the Origin's regained.
Since the music stopped, no shadow's touched
My door: again the village moon's above the river.

KOKAI (1403–69)

Only genuine awakening results in *that*.
Only fools seek sainthood for reward.
Lifting a hand, the stone lantern announces daybreak.
Smiling, the void nods its enormous head.

NENSHO (1409–82)

Unaware of illusion or enlightenment,
From this stone I watch the mountains, hear the stream.
A three-day rain has cleansed the earth,
A roar of thunder split the sky.
Ever serene are linked phenomena,
And though the mind's alert, it's but an ash heap.
Chilly, bleak as the dusk I move through,
I return, a basket brimmed with peaches on my arm.

GENKO (?–1505)

On Joshu's Nothingness

Earth, mountains, rivers—hidden in this nothingness.
In this nothingness—earth, mountains, rivers revealed.
Spring flowers, winter snows:
There's no being nor non-being, nor denial itself.

SAISHO (?–1506)

Why, it's but the motion of eyes and brows!
And here I've been seeking it far and wide.
Awakened at last, I find the moon
Above the pines, the river surging high.

YUISHUN (?–1544)

Though night after night
The moon is stream-reflected,
Try to find where it has touched,
Point even to a shadow.

TAKUAN (1573–1645)

It's not nature that upholds utility.
Look! even the rootless tree is swelled
With bloom, not red nor white, but lovely all the same.
How many can boast so fine a springtide?

GUDO (1579–1661)

Whirled by the three passions, one's eyes go blind;
Closed to the world of things, they see again.
In this way I live; straw-hatted, staff in hand,
I move illimitably, through earth, through heaven.

UNGO (1580–1659)

Here none think of wealth or fame,
All talk of right and wrong is quelled:
In autumn I rake the leaf-banked stream,
In spring attend the nightingale.

DAIGU (1584–1669)

Who dares approach the lion's
Mountain cave? Cold, robust,
A Zen-man through and through,
I let the spring breeze enter at the gate.

DAIGU

Unfettered at last, a traveling monk,
I pass the old Zen barrier.
Mine is a traceless stream-and-cloud life.
Of those mountains, which shall be my home?

MANAN (1591–1654)

Only the Zen-man knows tranquillity:
The world-consuming flame can't reach this valley.
Under a breezy limb, the windows of
The flesh shut firm, I dream, wake, dream.

FUGAI (17th century)

The moon's the same old moon,
The flowers exactly as they were,
Yet I've become the thingness
Of all the things I see!

BUNAN (1602–76)

When you're both alive and dead,
Thoroughly dead to yourself,
How superb
The smallest pleasure!

BUNAN

Beware of gnawing the ideogram of nothingness:
Your teeth will crack. Swallow it whole, and you've a treasure
Beyond the hope of Buddha and the Mind. The east breeze
Fondles the horse's ears: how sweet the smell of plum.

KARASUMARU-MITSUHIRO (1579–1638)

Content with chipped bowl and tattered robe,
My life moves on serenely.
The single task: allaying hunger, thirst,
Indifferent to the murmurous world.

TOSUI (?–1683)

The seven seas sucked up together,
The dragon god's exposed.
Backwards flows the stream of Soto Zen.
Enlightened at last, I breathe!

GESSHU (1618–96)

On Entering His Coffin
Never giving thought to fame,
One troublesome span of life behind,
Cross-legged in the coffin,
I'm about to slough the flesh.

BAIHO (1633–1707)

One minute of sitting, one inch of Buddha.
Like lightning all thoughts come and pass.
Just once look into your mind-depths:
Nothing else has ever been.

MANZAN (1635–1714)

The town's aflame with summer heat,
But Mount Koma is steeped in snow.
Such is a Zen-man's daily life—
The lotus survives all earthly fire.

TOKUO (1649–1709)

Past, present, future: unattainable,
Yet clear as the moteless sky.
Late at night the stool's cold as iron,
But the moonlit window smells of plum.

HAKUIN (1685–1768)

Priceless is one's incantation,
Turning a red-hot iron ball to butter oil.
Heaven? Purgatory? Hell?
Snowflakes fallen on the hearth fire.

HAKUIN

How lacking in permanence the minds of the sentient—
They are the consummate nirvana of all Buddhas.
A wooden hen, egg in mouth, straddles the coffin.
An earthenware horse breaks like wind for satori-land.

HAKUIN

You no sooner attain the great void
Than body and mind are lost together.
Heaven and Hell—a straw.
The Buddha-realm, Pandemonium—shambles.
Listen: a nightingale strains her voice, serenading the snow.
Look: a tortoise wearing a sword climbs the lampstand.
Should you desire the great tranquillity,
Prepare to sweat white beads.

HAKUIN

On Basho's "Frog"

Under the cloudy cliff, near the temple door,
Between dusky spring plants on the pond,
A frog jumps in the water, plop!
Startled, the poet drops his brush.

SENGAI (1750–1837)

Without a jot of ambition left
I let my nature flow where it will.
There are ten days of rice in my bag
And, by the hearth, a bundle of firewood.
Who prattles of illusion or nirvana?
Forgetting the equal dusts of name and fortune,
Listening to the night rain on the roof of my hut,
I sit at ease, both legs stretched out.

RYOKAN (1757–1831)

My hands released at last, the cliff soars
Ten thousand meters, the ploughshare sparks,
All's consumed with my body. Born again,
The lanes run straight, the rice well in the ear.

KANEMITSU-KOGUN (19th century)

A blind horse trotting up an icy ledge—
Such is the poet. Once disburdened
Of those frog-in-the-well illusions,
The sutra-store's a lamp against the sun.

KOSEN (1808–93)

Madness, the way they gallop off to foreign shores!
Turning to the One Mind, I find my Buddhahood,
Above self and others, beyond coming and going.
This will remain when all else is gone.

TANZAN (1819–92)

It's as if our heads were on fire, the way
We apply ourselves to perfection of That.
The future but a twinkle, beat yourself,
Persist: the greatest effort's not enough.

KANDO (1825–1904)

On New Year's Day
Fresh in their new wraps, earth and heaven,
And today I greet my eighty-first spring.
Ambition burning still, I grip my nandin staff.
Cutting through all, I spin the Wheel of Law.

NANTEMBO (1839–1925)

The question clear, the answer deep,
Each particle, each instant a reality,
A bird call shrills through mountain dawn:
Look where the old master sits, a rock, in Zen.

SODO (1841–1920)

On Climbing the Mountain Where Buddha Trained
However difficult the cliff,
It's only after climbing one's aware.
Leisurely I followed Tathagata's footsteps.
Roaring below, a tiger chilled the day.

MOKUSEN (1847–1920)

Calm, activity—each has its use. At times
This worldly dust piles mountain-high.
Now the neighbor's asleep, I chant a sutra.
The incense burnt away, I sing before the moon.

SOEN (1859–1919)

Master Joshu and the dog—
Truly exorbitant, their foolishness.
Being and non-being at last
Annihilated, speak the final word!

SOEN

On Visiting Shorin Temple,
Where Bodhidharma Once Lived
The steep slope hangs above
The temple calm. An autumn voyager,
I go by ways neither old nor new,
Finding east, west the mind the same.

SOEN

On Visiting Sokei,
Where the Sixth Patriarch Lived
The holy earth is overspread with leaves,
Wind crosses a thousand miles of autumn fields.
The moon that brushes Mount Sokei silvers,
This very instant, far Japan.

TESSHU (1879–1939)

Part Three

Japanese Haiku

To the willow—
all hatred, and desire
of your heart.
    BASHO (1644–94)

        Temple bell,
        a cloud of cherry flowers—
        Ueno? Asakusa?
            BASHO

Cormorant fishing:
how stirring,
how saddening.
    BASHO

        Year's end—
        still in straw hat
        and sandals.
            BASHO

Come, let's go
snow-viewing
till we're buried.
          BASHO

                              Come, see
                              real flowers
                              of this painful world.
                                        BASHO

Smell of autumn—
heart longs
for the four-mat room.
          BASHO

                              Skylark
                              sings all day,
                              and day not long enough.
                                        BASHO

Melon
in morning dew—
mud-fresh.
          BASHO

                              June rain,
                              hollyhocks turning
                              where sun should be.
                                        BASHO

Dozing on horseback,
smoke from tea-fires
drifts to the moon.
BASHO

Crow's
abandoned nest,
a plum tree.
BASHO

Journey's end—
still alive,
this autumn evening.
BASHO

Wintry day,
on my horse
a frozen shadow.
BASHO

Shrieking plovers,
calling darkness
around Hoshizaki Cape.
BASHO

Withered grass,
under piling
heat waves.
BASHO

Autumn moon,
tide foams
to the very gate.
        BASHO

Cedar umbrella,
off to Mount Yoshino
for the cherry blossoms.
        BASHO

Autumn—
even the birds
and clouds look old.
        BASHO

Year's end,
all corners
of this floating world, swept.
        BASHO

Buddha's death-day—
old hands
clicking rosaries.
        BASHO

To the capital—
snow-clouds forming,
half the sky to go.
        BASHO

Old pond,
leap-splash—
a frog.

BASHO

Girl cat,
so thin
on love and barley.

BASHO

Moor:
point my horse
where birds sing.

BASHO

Fish shop—
how cold the lips
of the salted bream.

BASHO

Autumn wind,
blasting the stones
of Mount Asama.

BASHO

Sick on a journey—
over parched fields
dreams wander on.

BASHO

Tomb, bend
to autumn wind—
my sobbing.
      BASHO

Summer grasses,
all that remains
of soldiers' dreams.
      BASHO

Full autumn moon—
on the straw mat,
pine shadow.
    KIKAKU (1661–1707)

Evening bridge,
a thousand hands
cool on the rail.
      KIKAKU

Sprinkle water wide—
for the sparrow,
the cicada.
      KIKAKU

Sacred night,
through masks
white breath of dancers.
      KIKAKU

Cicada chirp—
fan peddler
vaults a tree.
KIKAKU

Above the boat,
bellies
of wild geese.
KIKAKU

May he who brings
flowers tonight,
have moonlight.
KIKAKU

Summer airing—
trying on a quilt,
strutting around.
KIKAKU

Leaf
of the yam—
raindrop's world.
KIKAKU

Shrine gate
through morning mist—
a sound of waves.
KIKAKU

A sudden chill—
in our room my dead wife's
comb, underfoot.

   BUSON (1715–83)

     Dew on the bramble,
     thorns
     sharp white.

       BUSON

Through snow,
lights of homes
that slammed their gates on me.

    BUSON

     Ten holy nights—
     even tea
     chants *Namu Amida Butsu.*

       BUSON

My village—
dragonflies,
worn white walls.

   BUSON

     In sudden flare
     of the mosquito wick,
     her flushed face.

       BUSON

Happy traveler:
mosquito wick,
moonlit grasses.
BUSON

Wind in the west,
fallen leaves
gathering in the east.
BUSON

On the iris,
kite's
soft droppings.
BUSON

Short nap—
waking,
spring was gone.
BUSON

Miles of frost—
on the lake
the moon's my own.
BUSON

Over water,
sharp sickles
of reed gatherers.
BUSON

Mountains of Yoshino—
shedding petals,
swallowing clouds.

BUSON

Deer in rain—
three cries,
then heard no more.

BUSON

Swallows,
in eaves of mansions,
of hovels.

BUSON

Dewy morn—
these saucepans
are beautiful.

BUSON

Plum-viewing:
in the gay quarter
sashes are chosen.

BUSON

White lotus—
the monk
draws back his blade.

BUSON

Plum scent
haloing
the moon.

BUSON

Such a moon—
the thief
pauses to sing.

BUSON

In the melon-patch
thief, fox,
meet head-on.

TAIGI (1709–72)

Beyond serenity,
gray kites
in twilight.

TAIGI

Barley's season—
dust mutes
the midday bell.

TAIGI

Temple in
deep winter grove,
a bonfire's glow.

TAIGI

Zazen:
fat mosquitoes
everywhere.
                TAIGI

                In the boat,
                crescent moon's light
                in my lap.
                                TAIGI

Fallen leaves—
raking,
yet not raking.
                TAIGI

                Thunder—
                voices of drowned
                in sunken ships.
                                TAIGI

Swellfish eaten,
he chants *nembutsu*
in his sleep.
                TAIGI

                Cherry blossoms?
                In these parts
                grass also blooms.
                                ISSA (1763–1827)

Over paddies
at its foot,
smoke of Mount Asama.

ISSA

Changing clothes,
but not
the wanderer's lice.

ISSA

Owls are calling,
"Come, come,"
to the fireflies.

ISSA

Tonight you too
are rushed,
autumn moon.

ISSA

Just by being,
I'm here—
in snow-fall.

ISSA

Autumn wind,
the beggar looks
me over, sizing up.

ISSA

Lost in bamboo,
but when moon lights—
my house.

ISSA

Buddha Law,
shining
in leaf dew.

ISSA

A good world,
dew-drops fall
by ones, by twos.

ISSA

Listen,
all creeping things—
the bell of transience.

ISSA

Don't weep, insects—
lovers, stars themselves,
must part.

ISSA

Cuckoo sings
to me, to the mountain,
in turn.

ISSA

Flies swarming—
what do they want of
these wrinkled hands?

ISSA

One bath
after another—
how stupid.

ISSA

Where there are humans
you'll find flies,
and Buddhas.

ISSA

Farmer,
pointing the way
with a radish.

ISSA

Winter lull—
no talents,
thus no sins.

ISSA

Short night—
scarlet flower
at vine's tip.

ISSA

Let's take
the duckweed way
to clouds.

ISSA

Buddha's Nirvana,
beyond flowers,
and money.

ISSA

First cicada:
life is
cruel, cruel, cruel.

ISSA

Autumn evening—
knees in arms,
like a saint.

ISSA

At prayer,
bead-swinging
at mosquitoes.

ISSA

When plum
blooms—
a freeze in hell.

ISSA

Don't fly off, nightingale—
though your song's poor,
you're mine.

ISSA

Five yen each:
a cup of tea,
the nightingale.

ISSA

What a world,
where lotus flowers
are ploughed into a field.

ISSA

Fireflies
entering my house,
don't despise it.

ISSA

I'm leaving—
now you can make love,
my flies.

ISSA

Nightingale's song
this morning,
soaked with rain.

ISSA

Kites shriek
together—
departure of the gods.

ISSA

Children,
don't harm the flea,
with children.

ISSA

Borrowing my house
from insects,
I slept.

ISSA

Clouds of mosquitoes—
it would be bare
without them.

ISSA

About the field
crow moves
as if he's tilling.

ISSA

Autumn wind—
mountain's shadow
wavers.

ISSA

Watch it—you'll bump
your heads
on that stone, fireflies.
                    ISSA

                              My hut,
                              thatched
                              with morning glories.
                                            ISSA

Skylarks singing—
the farmer
makes a pillow of his hoe.
                    ISSA

                              Never forget:
                              we walk on hell,
                              gazing at flowers.
                                            ISSA

Outliving
them all, all—
how cold.
            ISSA

                              In this world
                              even butterflies
                              must earn their keep.
                                            ISSA

As we grow old,
what triumph
burning mosquitoes.

ISSA

Cuckoo's crying—
nothing special to do,
nor has the burweed.

ISSA

From the bough
floating down river,
insect song.

ISSA

Closer, closer
to paradise—
how cold.

ISSA

Worldly sky—
from now on
every year's a bonus.

ISSA

First firefly,
why turn away—
it's Issa.

ISSA

Under cherry trees
there are
no strangers.

ISSA

Be respectful,
sparrows,
of our old bedding.

ISSA

Dew spread,
the seeds of hell
are sown.

ISSA

Mokuboji Temple—
fireflies come even
to the barking dog.

ISSA

In my house
mice and fireflies
get along.

ISSA

Cries of wild geese,
rumors
spread about me.

ISSA

Shush, cicada—
old Whiskers
is about.

ISSA

Geese, fresh greens
wait for you
in that field.

ISSA

Treated shabbily
by fleas, by flies,
day quits.

ISSA

From burweed,
such a butterfly
was born?

ISSA

When I go,
guard my tomb well,
grasshopper.

ISSA

Reflected
in the dragonfly's eye—
mountains.

ISSA

A poor quarter:
flies, fleas, mosquitoes
live forever.

ISSA

No need to cling
to things—
floating frog.

JOSO (1662–1704)

About the grave
waves of spring mist—
I barely live.

JOSO

These branches
were the first to bud—
falling blossoms.

JOSO

Gruel heaped
in a perfect bowl—
sunlight of New Year's Day.

JOSO

How green—
flowering slopes
reflect each other.

JOSO

Writing,
rubbing it out—
face of poppy.
HOKUSHI (1665–1718)

My house gutted—
well, the cherry flowers
had fallen.

HOKUSHI

Sailboats in line,
island
lost in mist.
HOKUSHI

Woman—
how hot the skin
she covers.
LADY SUTE-JO (1633–98)

Are there
short-cuts in the sky,
summer moon?
LADY SUTE-JO

Contending—
temple bell,
winter wind.
KITO (1740–89)

Nightingale,
rarely seen,
came twice today.

KITO

Barley-reaping song,
smith's hammer,
mingling.

KITO

Seaweed
between rocks—
forgotten tides.

KITO

How cool,
forehead touched
to green straw-mat.

LADY SONO-JO (1649–1723)

Shameful
these clothes—
not one stitch mine.

LADY SONO-JO

After dream,
how real
the iris.

SHUSHIKI (1669–1725)

Frost of separation—
father, child
under one quilt.
                    SHUSHIKI

Even in my town
now, I sleep
like a traveler.
                    KYORAI (1651–1704)

After the green storm,
true color
of the rice-paddy.
                    KYORAI

Melon—
how well
it keeps itself.
                    RANSETSU (1654–1707)

Each morn
from the straw raincoat
put out to dry—fireflies.
                    RANSETSU

Traveling
old armor,
a glistening slug.
                    RANSETSU

Five rice dumplings
in bamboo leaves—
no message, no name.

RANSETSU

Fly, dare take
the rice grain
on my chin.

RANSETSU

Autumn wind—
across the fields,
faces.

ONITSURA (1660–1738)

Plum blossoms—
one's nose,
one's heart.

ONITSURA

Summer airing—
on one pole,
a shroud.

KYOROKU (1655–1715)

Even the dumplings
are smaller—
autumn wind.

KYOROKU

Night snow,
neighbor's cock
sounds miles away.
SHIKO (1665–1731)

Arid fields,
the only life—
necks of cranes.
SHIKO

Small fish-boats,
after what
as snow covers my hat?
SHIKO

First snow—
head clear,
I wash my face.
ETSUJIN (1656–1739)

Nightingale—
my clogs
stick in the mud.
BONCHO (?–1714)

Piled for burning,
brushwood
starts to bud.
BONCHO

Late spring:
paling rose,
bitter rhubarb.
SODO (1641–1716)

Sudden shower,
cooling lava
of Mount Asama.
SODO

Morning frost,
Mount Fuji
brushed lightly.
TANTAN (1674–1761)

On the rock
waves can't reach,
fresh snow.
TANTAN

Quivering together—
ears of barley,
butterfly.
LADY KANA-JO (17th century)

One sneeze—
skylark's
out of sight.
YAYU (1701–83)

Transplanting rice,
he pisses
in a crony's field.

YAYU

Whales
bellowing dawn,
in icy waters.

GYODAI (1732–93)

Inching
from dark to dark—
seaslug.

GYODAI

Slowly
over cedars,
sunshine, showers.

GYODAI

Forty years—
how sharp
the insect's cry.

SHIRAO (1735–92)

Mountain mist—
torches dropped
as clouds redden.

SHIRAO

Moonlit night—
by melon flowers,
fox sneezes.

SHIRAO

Were it not for
cries in snow,
would the herons be?

LADY CHIYO-JO (1701–75)

In the well-bucket,
a morning glory—
I borrow water.

LADY CHIYO-JO

Pure brush-clover—
basket of flowers,
basket of dew.

RYOTA (1707–87)

On rainy leaves
glow
of the village lights.

RYOTA

Tea-kettle,
hooked mid-air
towards heaven.

HAKUIN (1685–1768)

Cherry blossoms—
so many,
I'm bent over.
SOBAKU (1728–92)

Mirrored by stream,
swallow darts—
a fish.
SAIMARO (1656–1737)

Green, green, green—
herbs splash
the snow-field.
RAIZAN (1654–1716)

Cloud above lotus—
it too
becomes a Buddha.
BORYU (18th century)

Night frost—
pulsing wings
of mandarin ducks.
SOGI (1421–1502)

Cherry blossoms
dizzying—
my painful neck.
SOIN (1604–82)

Cold, yes,
but don't test
the fire, snow Buddha.
  SOKAN (1458–1546)

                              Nameless,
                              weed quickening
                              by the stream.
                              CHIUN (15th century)

Buddha:
cherry flowers
in moonlight.
HOITSU (1760–1828)

                              Moving
                              deep into mist,
                              chrysanthemums.
                              SAMPU (1647–1732)

Morning glory,
so pure
the dew's unseen.
KAKEI (1648–1716)

                              Chirping—
                              grasshopper
                              in the scarecrow's sleeve.
                              LADY CHIGETSU (17th century)

Spring plain,
gulped
by the pheasant's throat.
    YAMEI (18th century)

Long summer rains—
barley's tasteless
as the sky.
    MOKUSETSU (17th century)

Cry of the deer—
where at its depths
are antlers?
    OTSUYU (1674–1739)

Skylark
soaring—her young
will starve.
    SORA (1649–1710)

Wild geese—
fellow travelers,
all the way to Ise.
    LADY CHINE-JO (17th century)

Returning
by an unused path—
violets.
    BAKUSUI (1720–83)

My old thighs—
how thin
by firelight.
SHISEKI (1676–1759)

Shameful—
dead grass
in the insect's cage.
SHOHA (?–1771)

Guest gone,
I stroke the brazier,
talk to myself.
SHOZAN (1717–1800)

When bird passes on—
like moon,
a friend to water.
MASAHIDE (1657–1723)

Barn's burnt down—
now
I can see the moon.
MASAHIDE

Imagine—
the monk took off
before the moon shone.
SHIKI (1867–1902)

Thing long forgotten—
pot where a flower blooms,
this spring day.

SHIKI

Storm—chestnuts
race along
the bamboo porch.

SHIKI

Dew, clinging
to potato field,
the Milky Way.

SHIKI

Stone
on summer plain—
world's seat.

SHIKI

Autumn wind:
gods, Buddha—
lies, lies, lies.

SHIKI

Wicker chair
in pinetree's shade,
forsaken.

SHIKI

Aged nightingale—
how sweet
the cuckoo's cry.

SHIKI

Summer sky
clear after rain—
ants on parade.

SHIKI

Heath grass—
sandals
still fragrant.

SHIKI

Among Saga's
tall weeds,
tombs of fair women.

SHIKI

Evening bell:
persimmons pelt
the temple garden.

SHIKI

Autumn come—
cicada husk,
crackling.

SHIKI

Indian summer:
dragonfly shadows seldom
brush the window.

SHIKI

Midnight sound—
leap up:
a fallen moonflower.

SHIKI

Sudden rain—
rows of horses,
twitching rumps.

SHIKI

White butterfly
darting among pinks—
whose spirit?

SHIKI

Such silence:
snow tracing wings
of mandarin ducks.

SHIKI

Part Four

Shinkichi Takahashi (b. 1901), Contemporary Japanese Master

A Wood in Sound

The pine tree sways in the smoke,
Which streams up and up.
There's a wood in sound.

My legs lose themselves
Where the river mirrors daffodils
Like faces in a dream.

A cold wind and the white memory
Of a sasanqua.
Warm rain comes and goes.

I'll wait calmly on the bank
Till the water clears
And willows start to bud.

Time is singed on the debris
Of air raids.
Somehow, here and now, I am another.

Canna

A red canna blooms,
While between us flickers
A death's head, dancing there
Like a pigmy or tiny ball.

We try to catch it—
Now it brushes my hands,
Now dallies with her feet.

She often talks of suicide.
Scared, I avoid her cold face.

Again today she spoke
Of certain premonitions.
How can I possibly
Save this woman's life?

Living as if dead, I shall
Give up my own. She must live.

Thistles

Thistles bloomed in the vast moonlit
Cup of the Mexican sands.

Thistles bloomed on the round hillock
Of a woman's heart.

The stained sea was choked with thistles,
Sky stowed away in thistle stalks.

Thistles, resembling a male corpse, bloomed
Like murex from a woman's side.

At the thorny root of a yellow cactus plant
A plucked pigeon crouched,

And off in the distance a dog whimpered,
As if swallowing hot air.

Burning Oneself to Death

That was the best moment of the monk's life.
Firm on a pile of firewood
With nothing more to say, hear, see,
Smoke wrapped him, his folded hands blazed.

There was nothing more to do, the end
Of everything. He remembered, as a cool breeze
Streamed through him, that one is always
In the same place, and that there is no time.

Suddenly a whirling mushroom cloud rose
Before his singed eyes, and he was a mass
Of flame. Globes, one after another, rolled out,
The delighted sparrows flew round like fire balls.

The Pipe

While I slept it was all over,
Everything. My eyes, squashed white,
Flowed off toward dawn.

There was a noise,
Which, like all else, spread and disappeared:
There's nothing worth seeing, listening for.

When I woke, everything seemed cut off.
I was a pipe, still smoking,
Which daylight would knock empty once again.

Destruction

The universe is forever falling apart—
No need to push the button,
It collapses at a finger's touch:
Why, it barely hangs on the tail of a sparrow's eye.

The universe is so much eye secretion,
Hordes leap from the tips
Of your nostril hairs. Lift your right hand:
It's in your palm. There's room enough
On the sparrow's eyelash for the whole.

A paltry thing, the universe:
Here is all strength, here the greatest strength.
You and the sparrow are one
And, should he wish, he can crush you.
The universe trembles before him.

What Is Moving

When I turned to look back
Over the waters
The sky was birdless.

Men *were, are* born.
Do I still live? I ask myself,
Munching a sweet potato.

Don't smell of death,
Don't cast its shadow.
Any woman when I glance her way,
Looks down,
Unable to stand it.
Men, as if dead,
Turn up the whites of their eyes.

Get rid of those trashy ideas—
The same thing
Runs through both of us.
My thought moves the world:
I move, it moves.
I crook my arm, the world's crooked.

The Peach

A little girl under a peach tree,
Whose blossoms fall into the entrails
Of the earth.

There you stand, but a mountain may be there
Instead; it is not unlikely that the earth
May be yourself.

You step against a plate of iron and half
Your face is turned to iron. I will smash
Flesh and bone

And suck the cracked peach. She went up the mountain
To hide her breasts in the snowy ravine.
Women's legs

Are more or less alike. The leaves of the peach tree
Stretch across the sea to the end of
The continent.

The sea was at the little girl's beck and call.
I will cross the sea like a hairy
Caterpillar

And catch the odor of your body.

Quails

It is the grass that moves, not the quails.
Weary of embraces, she thought of
Committing her body to the flame.

When I shut my eyes, I hear far and wide
The air of the Ice Age stirring.
When I open them, a rocket passes over a meteor.

A quail's egg is complete in itself,
Leaving not room enough for a dagger's point.
All the phenomena in the universe: myself.

Quails are supported by the universe
(I wonder if that means subsisting by God).
A quail has seized God by the neck

With its black bill, because there is no
God greater than a quail.
(Peter, Christ, Judas: a quail.)

A quail's egg: idle philosophy in solution.
(There is no wife better than a quail.)
I dropped a quail's egg into a cup for buckwheat noodles,

And made havoc of the Democratic Constitution.
Split chopsticks stuck in the back, a quail husband
Will deliver dishes on a bicycle, anywhere.

The light yellow legs go up the hill of Golgotha.
Those quails who stood on the rock, became the rock!
The nightfall is quiet, but inside the congealed exuviae

Numberless insects zigzag, on parade.

Rain

The rain keeps falling,
Even in dreams.
The skull leaks badly.

There's a constant dripping
Down the back.
The rain, which no one

Remembers starting,
Keeps falling,
Even on the finest days.

The Position of the Sparrow

The sparrow has cut the day in half:
Afternoons—yesterday's, the day after tomorrow's—
Layer the white wall.
Those of last year, and next year's too,
Are dyed into the wall—see them?—
And should the wall come down,
Why, those afternoons will remain,
Glimmering, just as they are, through time.
(That was a colorless realm where,
Nevertheless, most any color could well up.)

Just as the swan becomes a crow,
So everything improves—everything:
No evil *can* persist, and as to things,
Why, nothing is unchangeable.
The squirrel, for instance, is on the tray,
Buffalos lumber through African brush,
The snail wends along the wall,
Leaving a silver trail.
The sparrow's bill grips a pomegranate seed:
Just anything can resemble a lens, or a squirrel.

Because the whole is part, there's not a whole,
Anywhere, that is not part.
And all those happenings a billion years ago,
Are happening now, all around us: time.
Indeed this morning the sparrow hopped about
In that nebulous whirlpool
A million light years hence.
And since the morning is void,
Anything can be. Since mornings
A billion years from now are nothingness,
We can behold them.
The sparrow stirs,
The universe moves slightly.

Stitches

My wife is always knitting, knitting:
Not that I watch her,
Not that I know what she thinks.

(Awake till dawn
I drowned in your eyes—
I must be dead:
Perhaps it's the mind that stirs.)

With that bamboo needle
She knits all space, piece by piece,
Hastily hauling time in.

Brass-cold, exhausted,
She drops into bed and,
Breathing calmly, falls asleep.

Her dream must be deepening,
Her knitting coming loose.

Fish

I hold a newspaper, reading.
Suddenly my hands become cow ears,
Then turn into Pusan, the South Korean port.

Lying on a mat
Spread on the bankside stones,
I fell asleep.
But a willow leaf, breeze-stirred,
Brushed my ear.
I remained just as I was,
Near the murmurous water.

When young there was a girl
Who became a fish for me.
Whenever I wanted fish
Broiled in salt, I'd summon her.
She'd get down on her stomach
To be sun-cooked on the stones.
And she was always ready!

Alas, she no longer comes to me.
An old benighted drake,
I hobble homeward.
But look, my drake feet become horse hoofs!
Now they drop off
And, stretching marvelously,
Become the tracks of the Tokaido Railway Line.

Afterimages
The volcanic smoke of Mount Aso
Drifted across the sea, white ash
Clinging to mulberry leaves
And crowning the heads of sparrows.

An open-mouthed lava crocodile;
A sparrow like a fossil sprig,
The moon filling its eyes;
A colossal water lizard stuck to a dead tree,
Its headland tail quaking.

A cloud floats in my head—beautiful!
When the sparrow opens its eyes,
Nothing but rosy space. All else gone.

Don't tell me that tree was red—
The only thing that moved, ever closer,
Was a girl's nose. All mere afterimages.

Water, coldness itself, flows underfoot.

The sparrow, eyes half closed, lay in an urn
In the pit. Now it fans up. The earth's
Fiery column is nearly extinguished.

Shell

Nothing, nothing at all
    is born,
dies, the shell says again
    and again
from the depth of hollowness.
    Its body
swept off by tide—so what?
    It sleeps
in sand, drying in sunlight,
    bathing
in moonlight. Nothing to do
    with sea
or anything else. Over
    and over
it vanishes with the wave.

Mushroom

I blow tobacco smoke
into her frozen ear.
A swallow darts above.

Pleasures are like mushrooms,
rootless, flowerless,
shoot up anywhere.

A metal ring hangs
from her ear, mildew
glowing in the dark.

Flight of the Sparrow
Sparrow dives from roof to ground,
a long journey—a rocket soars
to the moon, umpteen globes collapse.

Slow motion: twenty feet down, ten billion
years. Light-headed, sparrow does not think,
philosophize, yet all's beneath his wings.

What's Zen? "Thought," say masters,
"makes a fool." How free the brainless
sparrow. Chirrup—before the first "chi,"

a billion years. He winks, another. Head left,
mankind's done. Right, man's born again.
So easy, there's no end to time.

One gulp, swallow the universe. Flutter
on limb or roof—war, peace, care banished.
Nothing remains—not a speck.

"Time's laid out in the eavestrough,"
sparrow sings,
                pecks now and then.

Sky
Climbing the wax tree
to the thundering sky,
I stick my tongue out—
what a downpour!

Sparrow in Withered Field
Feet pulled in, sparrow dead
under a pall of snow.
"Sparrow's a red-black bird,"
someone says, then—
"sun's a white-winged bird."

If the bird sleeps, so will man:
things melt in air, there's only breathing.
You're visible, nose to feet,
and while an ant guard rams a 2-by-4
genitals saunter down the road.

Budge them, they'll roll over—
pour oil on them, light up.

Atom of thought, ten billion years—
one breath, past, present, future.

Wood's so quiet. I cover my ears—
how slowly the universe crumbles.

Snow in withered field, nothing to touch.
Sparrow's head clear as sky.

Afternoon
My hair's falling fast—
this afternoon
I'm off to Asia Minor.

Hand
I stretch my hand—
everything disappears.

I saw in the snake-head
my dead mother's face,

in ragged clouds
grief of my dead father.

Snap my fingers—
time's no more.

My hand's the universe,
it can do anything.

Sweet Potato
Of all things living
I'd be a sweet potato,
fresh dug up.

Camel
The camel's humps
shifted with clouds.

Such solitude beheads!
My arms stretch

beyond mountain peaks,
flame in the desert.

Raw Fish and Vegetables

When unborn, my mother minced
time with her rusty knife—
rain-soft, grained like cod-roe.
When ready, I burst from her womb.

Nothing better to do, I try
to relive that first house:
no one else there, however I
kicked touching nothing in
darkness—mite in a whale.

Posterity aeons hence, listen:
time's a white radish, pickled,
yellowing. My father swam that
vinegar's raw fish and vegetables.

Downy Hair

Charmed by a girl's soft ears,
I piled up leaves and burnt them.

How innocent her face
in rising smoke—I longed

to roam the spiral of those ears,
but she clung stiffly

to the tramcar strap, downy
hair fragrant with leafsmoke.

Toad
"The instant he boarded the plane
Toad was in London"—wrong.

Toad's unaware of distance,
between his belly and man's,
between himself, the crushing wheel.

"Shrinking utterly, he's nowhere"—right.

London, Tokyo flattened by webbed feet
all at once. In the marsh—no distance, sound—
a scaly back is overgrown with moonflowers.

Drizzle
Cat runs the dripping fence,
melts into green shade
hollow as thought lost.

Earth in a claw of dead cat,
guts strewn on pavement—
time, those needle eyes.

In the garret three kittens lap.
An old woman, like a crumpled bill,
tries to recall cat's name.

Sea of Oblivion
Future, past, the sea
of oblivion,
with present capsized.

Sun splits the sea
in two—
one half's already bottled.

Legs spread on the beach,
a woman feels
the crab of memory

crawl up her thigh.
Somewhere
her lover drowns.

Sand-smeared, bathing
in dreams,
the young leap against each other.

Cloud
I'm cheerful, whatever happens,
a puff in sky—
what splendor exists, I'm there.

Mother and I
While boats list in port
sunset ripens
the forest of Hakone.

Men fall like raindrops.
I perch on
a chair, open my umbrella.

Cloud-burst. Smiling, mother
sits up in
her coffin. Ages ago.

Tomorrow Columbus will reach
(was it?)
Venezuela, this hand

will embrace or kill—takes
but a finger.
Under white sail, the universe.

Sheep

Awaking on grass, sheep, goat
stay put—how fine doing nothing,
Crow points from dead branch.

Sheep could care less—life, death,
all one where she lies
soft warm wool. Goat bleats,

horns sun-tipped. What's better
than warmth? sheep muses, sharing
her wonder with goat, with crow.

Eternity

Ice on eaves, sparrow melts in my head,
cracked shapeless, no hint of brain.

Sparrow's long journey. Now road flowers,
young girls breasting wheat.

(Once fry shot upstream towards clouds.)

Sparrow blinked: drifting on the moonlit sea,
a woman, legs octopus arms, waves biting

to black eyes. No need to grasp, no rim,
depth, shallowness—sun's steering

round the navel, galaxies whirl the spine.
Snow's hip-high, thighs stiff with frost.

(Sweet as fish, how fresh death's breeze.)

Sparrow and Bird-Net Building
Sparrow's always sleeping—
meanwhile
a building surrounds him.

Snoop, shoot up the
elevator,
quite alone: the building's

a pinch of dust. No day,
night,
so light strikes from

his throat, under a wing
glow
sun, moon, stars. No one's here,

no one's expected for a billion
years.
Sparrow dreams, sparrow knows.

Clay Image
Near the shrine, humped back,
bird on pole—eyes, warm
as folded wings, reflect
the penumbra of the universe.

On the horizon,
a cylindrical building,
once bird, now mud and stone.

Birth's a crack in the
ground plan. Since universe
is no bigger than its head,
where's the bird to fly?

Who says bird's eyelashes
are short? A lump,
time rolled from nostril.

Cooling the bird's hot tongue,
the unglazed red clay image.

Its eyes dark, and in their
cavities—
minute vibrations, earthquakes.

Gods
Gods are everywhere:
war between Koshi and Izumo
tribes still rages.

The all of All, the One
ends distinctions.

The three thousand worlds
are in that plum blossom.
The smell is God.

Braggart Duck
Duck lives forever,
daily. Waking, he finds
he's slept a billion years.

The very center of the
universe, he has no use
for eyes, ears, feet.

What need for one
who knows his world
of satellite stations?

Freed from time,
changeless. Duck's not
sharp as dog shooting

through space, a rocket.
Besides he's
been there already.

Stone Wall

Flower bursts from stone,
in rain and wind
dog sniffs and aims a leak.
Butterfly-trace through haze
where child splashes.

Over the paper screen,
a woman's legs, white, fast.
No more desire, I'm content.

Later I saw her, hands
behind her back—
repulsing nothing really,
welcoming sun
between her thighs.

Near the stone wall,
a golden branch.

Beach

Gale: tiles, roofs whirling,
disappearing at once.

Rocks rumble, mountains
swallow villages,
yet insects, birds chirp by
the shattered bridge.

Men shoot through space,
race sound. On TV nations
maul each other, endlessly.

Why this confusion,
how restore the ravaged
body of the world?

Moon and Hare

Things exist alone.
Up on the moon
I spot Hare

in a crater
pounding rice to cakes.
I ask for one.

"What shape?" says Hare.
"One like a rocket."
"Here—take off!"

Up and out,
pass everything
at once,

free at last—
unaware of
where I'm heading.

Lap Dog

Lap dog in a cloth-wrapped box,
moist eyes, nose,
I tote you in place
of your evaporated mistress.

I'd like to brew down, devour,
ten thousand mini-skirted legs.

Body torn, yet spirit's whole,
no knife can reach it.
Dawn breaks from her buttocks.

Runaway tramcar thunders by,
sun-flash! Fling
the lap dog down a manhole.

Ha! Sun-blade's in her back.

Moon

Moon shines while billions
of corpses rot
beneath earth's crust.
I who rise from them,
soon to join them—all.
Where does moon float?
On the waves of my brain.

Vimalakirti

Vimalakirti, Vaishali
millionaire, sutra hero,
in bed in his small space—

while you're sick,
I'll lie here.
Revive, I'm whole.

Illness, a notion,
for him body is sod, water—
moves, a fire, a wind.

Vimalakirti, layman hero,
at a word draws galaxies
to the foot of his bed.

Snowy Sky

The blackbird swooped,
eyes shadowing earth, dead leaves,
feathers tipped with snow.

One finds beaches anywhere,
airports, skies of snow.

Perched on the ticket counter,
blackbird watches
the four-engined plane land,
propellers stilled.

Dead leaves flutter from the sky.

Near Shinobazu Pond

A bream swam by the tramcar window,
the five-tiered pagoda bright in rain.

On the telephone wire, sparrow—
amused, in secret dialogue.

Voiceless, rock glimmers with
a hundred million years.

Day before yesterday, the dead sparrow
hopped on the fish-tank

where froth-eyed salamander
and a tropic fish curled fins.

The sparrow, spot of rose among
the lotus leaves, stirs evening air.

Let's Live Cheerfully
Dead man steps over sweaty sleepers
on the platform, in quest of peace.

Thunderously dawn lights earth.

Smashed by the train, head spattered
on the track—not a smudge of brain.

Nothing left: thought—smoke.
A moment—a billion years.

Don't curl like orange peel, don't ape
a mummified past. Uncage eternity.

When self's let go, universe is all—
O for speed to get past time!

Rocks
Because the stake was driven
in that rice paddy,
world was buried in mud.

Rocks dropped like birds
from the crater:
being is mildew spread on non-being.

Rocks that were women stand,
wooden stakes, everywhere,
give birth to stones.

No-minds—whirling, flying off, birds.

Urn

Autumn blast—wild boar
limps, one leg dead grass.
Bird sings, feathers tattered,
eyes stiff twigs.
Boar gives his own.

As those bronze cavities
decay, he fuses into rock,
sets it and bird to flame,
and meteors to the sky.

Boar flashes on the sun,
red tail severed, scorching:
urn, inlaid with gold
and silver, holds the image.

Through night, glittering
with millet seeds,
boar shoots, a comet.

Spring

Spring one hundred years ago
was very warm: it's in my
palm, such life, such gaiety.

Future is a bird streaking
aimlessly, past is dregs—
everything's here, now.

Thought sparking thought
sparking thought: headlands
pocked by time, the ram of tides.

Rock rising, rock sinking.
No space, what was is nowhere—
a hundred years hence,

spring will be as warm.

Peach Blossom and Pigeon
(painting by Kiso)
Pink petals of peach blossom,
blue/green pigeon's head,

eyes bamboo slits, rainbow
wings fold in all history.

Black tail down, you fly to
future's end, beyond the sun.

To clear the air, make sweetest
scent, you bulge your breast.

Branch in your coffee-colored claws,
wait till phantom bubbles burst around.

Spinning Dharma Wheel
A stone relief I never tire of:
life-sized Buddha, broken nose,
hair spiraling, eyes serene moons,
chipped mudra-fingers at the breast,
legs crossed in lotus. Under each arm
a red line streams—warm blood.
Around the halo, angels among flowers,
on either side, beasts, open-mouthed,
on guard. He turns the treasure wheel.
Three thousand years since Buddha
found the morning star—now
sun itself is blinded by his light.

Four Divine Animals

Snake swam across the blue stream.
You've seen its slough—your own?

Tiger in the white bamboo, eyes hard:
learn from this—to see death
is to see another, never oneself.

Flames char the bamboo grove,
the vermilion sparrow has flown
into a fossil—just like that.

Tortoise moves, a slow fire,
down hill, flushed in sunset—
claws death to shreds, red, brown.

Tiger's soft tongue laps a dragon
from the sea. Sparrow, riding
a shell-tank, makes for its belly.

What's this? My body's shaking with laughter.

A Little Sunlight

Trees in the wood lifeless,
leaves pall the earth.
On a large drift the red-sweatered

woman waits. There's just
a blink of sun, a leaf blows
on her face. The man comes up

quietly, lies down beside her.
Soon she takes off alone,
toting her case. He prays

(I hear him now) all may go well
with her. A plane roars above,
he snuffs his cigarette.

Two dead leaves blow apart.

Explosion

I'm an unthinking dog,
a good-for-nothing cat,
a fog over gutter,
a blossom-swiping rain.

I close my eyes, breathe—
radioactive air! A billion years
and I'll be shrunk to half,
pollution strikes my marrow.

So what—I'll whoop at what
remains. Yet scant blood left,
reduced to emptiness by nuclear
fission, I'm running very fast.

Railroad Station

A railroad station, a few
passengers getting on, off,
a closed stall on the platform.

Is it there or in my head,
floating on the creases
of my brain? No need to stay

or leave, a place so quiet:
ticket window, wicket, employees—
none. But there's a samurai

committing suicide. Station
master cocks the camera's eye,
proof of his diligence.

Train skims rails of my brain,
what's hanging to that strap
is briefcase, camera, no man.

Absence
Just say, "He's out"—
back in
five billion years!

Afterword
Death of a Zen Poet:
Shinkichi Takahashi (1901–1987)

⁓⁂⁓

It was one of those moments one stands outside one's body, staring at the silhouette, dumbstruck, not wanting to believe words coming in. The phoned message from Japan was that the greatest modern Zen poet had died. I waited for the eulogies, a voice to cry out at the passing of a man who made fresh visions of the world, made wild and powerful music out of anything: shells, knitting, peaches, an airplane passing between his legs, the sweet-sour smell coming from a cemetery of unknown soldiers, the crab of memory crawling up a woman's thigh, a sparrow whose stir can move the universe. A man who showed that things loved or despised were, when all's said and done, as important and unimportant as each other. But all was silence as I looked out, hoping for a cloud of his beloved sparrows bearing his karma wheel around the earth.

I realized that he might prefer it this way. Yet there remain the masterworks, his gift to us, in spite of his mixed feelings on the handing down of insight with mere words. "If we sit in Zen at all," he says in the foreword to *Afterimages,* a collection of his poems, "we must model ourselves on the Bodhidharma, who kept sitting till his buttocks grew rotten. We must have done with all words and letters, and attain Truth itself. As a follower of the tradition of Zen which is above verbalization, I must confess that I feel ashamed of writing poems and having collections of them published. My wish is that through books like this the West will awake to the Buddha's Truth. It is my belief that Buddhism will travel round the world till it will bury its old bones in the ridges of the Himalayas."

Yet, paradoxically, Shinkichi Takahashi was one of Japan's most prolific poets, greatly honored (his *Collected Poems* won the Ministry of Education's Prize for Art), thought by the Japanese to be their only poet who could properly be called a Zen poet, for his practice of the discipline was exceptionally pure. He discovered early in life that unless he grappled with the severest of the doctrine's principles he would not be living, or writing, worthily. Yet, stuffy as this sounds, there was much humor in him, as in all enlightened Zenists:

Afternoon
My hair's falling fast—
this afternoon
I'm off to Asia Minor.

The Pink Sun
White petals on the black earth,
Their scent filling her nostrils.

Breathe out and all things swell—
Breathe in, they shrink.

Let's suppose she suddenly has four legs—
That's far from fantastic.

I'll weld ox hoofs onto her feet—
Sparks of the camellia's sharp red.

Wagging her pretty little tail,
She's absorbed in kitchen work.

Look, she who just last night
Was a crone is girl again,

An alpine rose blooming on her arm.
High on a Himalayan ridge

The great King of Bhutan
Snores in the pinkest sun.

The poet, born in 1901 in a fishing village on Shikoku, smallest of Japan's four main islands, was largely self-educated, but broadly so: writing extensively on many aspects of Japanese culture, he introduced an important series of art books and had a successful career as a man of letters. Not bad for one who had dropped out of high school and rushed off to Tokyo in hope of a literary career. There he contracted typhus and, penniless, landed in a charity hospital. His circumstances forced him to return to his village. But one day, fired up by a newspaper article on dadaism, he returned to Tokyo, working as a waiter in a *shiruko* restaurant (*shiruko* is red-bean soup with bits of rice cake) and as a "pantry boy" in a newspaper office, running errands and serving tea.

In 1923 he brought out *Dadaist Shinkichi's Poetry*. The first copy of it was handed him through the bars of a police cell—at this time he was often in trouble for impulsive actions—and he tore it up without so much as a glance. Other collections followed, but by 1928 he knew his life was in dire need of guidance, and like many troubled artists he sought the advice of a Zen master. He could not have chosen better. Shizan Ashikaga, illustrious Rinzai Zen master of the Shogen Temple, was known to be a disciplinarian, one not likely to be impressed by a disciple's literary forays.

At first the toughness of the training proved too much. Pacing the temple corridor, he fell unconscious; when he came to, he was incoherent. Later he was to write that this was inevitable, considering how completely different ascetic exercises were from his daily life and with what youthful single-mindedness he had pursued them. He was sent back to his family and virtually locked up in a small (two-mat) room for three long years. During this confinement he wrote many poems, which may have helped him to survive the ordeal and recover.

Back in Tokyo in 1932, Takahashi began attending Master Shizan Ashikaga's lectures on Zen. Shizan once cautioned him, "Attending lectures cuts no ice. Koan exercise [meditation on Zen problems set by a master] is all-important." Takahashi became his disciple in 1935. During almost seventeen years of rigorous training he experienced both great hardships and exultations of satori. By 1951, having learned all that he could, he was given, in the master's own calligraphy, "The Moon-on-Water Hall"—his *inka,* or testimony that he had successfully completed the full course of discipline, one of only seven over many years so honored by the master.

Takahashi visited Korea and China in 1939 and was deeply impressed by Zenists he met there. He lived chiefly by his writings, and in 1944 began work for a Tokyo newspaper, leaving when its office was bombed out in 1945. He married in 1951 and lived with his wife and their two daughters in great serenity, a life he scarcely could have dreamt of in his turbulent youth.

The poet had distinguished himself in many ways by the time the first translated collection of his poems, *Afterimages,* appeared (simultaneously in the United States and England in 1970) to much acclaim. A reviewer in the *Hudson Review* observed that while other poets, East and West, would appear to descend from time to time into the natural world, Takahashi would emerge from it like a seal from the depths of the sea, his constant element. But it wasn't sea or nature the poet lived in, it was Zen.

Yet that would hardly account for the appeal of his work, especially among fellow poets, throughout the world, with or without interest in Zen. He was foremost an artist. Many aestheticians have spoken of the difficulty of defining art, yet some artists have on occasion chosen to speak out, as did Tolstoy in *What Is*

Art? Tolstoy identified three essential ingredients of effective art—individuality, clarity and sincerity—and to the degree that each, in combination with the others, was present, a work could be ranked on a scale of merely acceptable to necessary. Tolstoy was a moralist in all such matters, and never tired of inveighing against aesthetic notions based largely on the pleasure principle, among them "art for art's sake"—life was too serious for such twaddle.

Though as a Zenist Takahashi was not inclined to theorize on literary matters, he might well have agreed with Tolstoy. Surely none would question the sincerity (integrity?) of his work, and that it should be individual, as all true Zen art, is perhaps axiomatic. It is the remaining essential in Tolstoy's triad, clarity, that some may claim is critically missing. But as the poet often said, the very nature of the Zen pursuit, the attainment of spiritual awakening, rules out likelihood of easy accessibility to its arts. "When I write poems," he told me, "no allowances can be made. Thought of a poem's difficulty never troubles me, since I never consciously make poems difficult."

A major reason for the difficulty of Zen poems, throughout the fifteen hundred years they have been written, is that many, perhaps the best known and most valued in and out of Zen communities, are those of "mutual understanding" (*agyo* or *toki-no-ge* in Japanese). Such poems are basically koan interpretations, as is the following piece, "Collapse," written by Takahashi early in Zen training:

Time oozed from my pores,
Drinking tea
I tasted the seven seas.

I saw in the mist formed
Around me
The fatal chrysanthemum, myself.

Its scent choked, and as I
Rose, squaring
My shoulders, the earth collapsed.

This, Takahashi told me, was written in response to a koan
his master asked him to meditate on, one often given disciples
early in training, "Describe your face before you were begotten by
your parents." We observe the poet deep in *zazen* (formal Zen
meditation), experiencing the extraordinary expansions and pene-
trations sometimes realized by the meditator. Suddenly, in the
mist, he sees that face and is repulsed ("Its scent choked"). He
rises, freed from it, ready for anything. The old world breaks up,
and he enters the new.

Though Takahashi was always forthcoming with me about
circumstances that may have led to the making of such poems (I
was, after all, his translator), he was reluctant to reveal the manner
in which they were received by the master, feeling such revela-
tions would be too intimate. That attitude is only natural, per-
haps, and besides, Zenists are cautioned to avoid such dis-
closures. The poet did confide, however, that the following was
his versification of the master's response to one of his koan-
based poems:

Words

I don't take your words
Merely as words.
Far from it.

I listen
To what makes you talk—
Whatever that is—
And me listen.

It is intriguing to imagine the scene: poet sitting before master for *sanzen* (a meeting for discussion of progress with koan), daring to complain that his interpretive poem was being misunderstood. "Words," expressing more than gentle reproach, relates intimately to a special bond, while at the same time it defines perhaps the nature of such talk, in or out of a *zendo* (meditation hall). As one might suppose, there are no correct interpretations. The koan is meant to dislodge, throw off balance, and the adequate poem reveals to what degree the disciple has righted himself— nothing more or less. And the more successful the interpretation, the finer the poem as poem.

The poem of mutual understanding, important to Zen since the T'ang dynasty, is a clear gauge of progress in discipline. It is not "poem" until such judgment is made, not by a literary critic but by a qualified master. Most awakening poems are of this type, though hardly planned or anticipated. Only a master, aware of his disciple's needs, lacks and strengths, knows whether the longed-for breakthrough has been made. The poem tells all, accompanied of course by numerous signs in conduct itself, in speech, walk, work and relationship with others.

The Japanese master Daito (1282–1337), when a disciple, was given by his master the eighth koan of *Hekiganroku,* a Chinese work of great antiquity made up of one hundred Zen problems with commentary. Daito, who gained satori from his struggle with the koan, wrote at least two poems of mutual understanding based on it. Here is the text of the koan and the two most important poems it inspired:

Attention! Suigan, at the end of the summer, spoke to the assembly and said: "For the whole summer I have lectured to the brethren. Look! Has Suigan any eyebrows?" Hofuko said, "He who does robberies has a heart of deceit." Chokei said, "They grow." Unmon said, "A barrier!"

Unmon's barrier pulled down, the old
Path lost. Blue sky's my home,
My every action beyond man's reach:
A golden priest, arms folded, has returned.

At last I've broken Unmon's barrier!
There's exit everywhere—east, west; north, south.
In at morning, out at evening; neither host nor guest.
My every step stirs up a little breeze.

Not all awakening poems are written in response to koan.
Often a master, in normal conversation, will unconsciously chal-
lenge disciples to grapple with more general things. The subject
of Time is much discussed in Zen communities. Takahashi once
told me that the following lines came about that way.

Time

Time like a lake breeze
Touched his face.
All thought left his mind.

One morning the sun, menacing,
Rose from behind a mountain,
Singeing—like hope—the trees.

Fully awakened, he lit his pipe
And assumed the sun-inhaling pose:
Time poured down—like rain, like fruit.

He glanced back and saw a ship
Moving toward the past. In one hand
He gripped the sail of eternity,

And stuffed the universe into his eyes.

The American poet Richard Ronan, in his master's thesis, "Process and Mastery in Bashō and Wallace Stevens," dealt most convincingly with this and other Takahashi poems. He wrote:

> The "lake breeze" is an allusion to the Hindu concept of *nirvana,* literally to be "blown away," a concept from which the Japanese satori, enlightenment, is derived. Reaching *nirvana/satori,* one's relativity is necessarily blown away, leaving only one's essential nature, which is identical to that of the Void, the Buddhist Absolute. Having conquered the sun of Time, the speaker inhales it, absurdly smoking his pipe. He consumes the universe by seeing it for the first time as it is. "Devouring time" is devoured by the poet's *satori* conquest of the relative.

The conquest of the relative, the leap from the conditioned to an unconditioned plateau of being, is the extraordinary goal of Zen, and it is the reigning paradox of Zen art that work so private, of "mutual understanding," should have such broad appeal. In order for the Zenist to take the leap, he must attain a state of no-mind (*wu-hsin* in Chinese)—"All thought left his mind" in Takahashi's "Time"—an essential precondition of *muga,* the full identification of observer and observed. The aesthetic term *zenkan* (pure seeing) has application to all Zen arts, and what it implies about the practitioner is startling: somehow he has won through, crushed the hungering ego, which in the unenlightened bars realization. The true Zen artist, of whatever medium, is a man risen from that smoldering.

Among modern poets, East and West, Shinkichi Takahashi was distinguished largely through the practice of *zenkan,* identifying effortlessly with all he observed, through which he ennobled not only his art but life itself. Like all awakened Zenists he found no separation between art and life, knowing the achievement of no-mind led not only to right art but to right living. He rarely used such general terms, but on occasion would explain what the practice of *zenkan* had meant to him. As an artist, he had engaged for years in intense, unobstructed observation. Things moving, stationary; one no more appropriate than another, no circumstance more or less favorable. He always cautioned, as he himself had been, against dualism, assuring that little by little one learns to know true seeing from false, that it was possible to reach the unconditioned. The world, he claimed, is always pure—we, with our dripping mind-stuff, foul it.

So puzzling to most of us. In the West some—Paul Valéry for one—without reference to Zen or other disciplines, turned in horror from the shifting mind, all a-wobble, twisted this way and that, filled with anxieties. Such men have spoken out of the need to subdue the mind, crush the ego, but where have they offered the way to make that possible? We don't appreciate how wise we are when we speak of troubles being "only in the mind," for born and heavily nourished there, they become giants that slay. When emptied of them and pointed properly, the mind is no longer a destructive agent: it is the only light we need. Zen has been saying this for fifteen hundred years, never more effectively than through its poets, among whom in our lifetime Shinkichi Takahashi was the most profound.

I last saw the poet in the summer of 1985. He had insisted on postponing entering the hospital so that we might meet at his home in Tokyo. Ten years had passed since our last meeting, in the very same room. Though much changed, so weak he could not stand, there was the same vitality in his voice, the old sparkle in his eyes. In the past we had met chiefly to discuss his poems, pieces I was attempting with Takashi Ikemoto's help to render into English. Now we laughed together with his gentle wife, remembering old moments. When a common friend took out a camera, he begged him not to waste the film on him but to instead photograph his *inka* framed on the wall. Suddenly he looked up, smiled at me and said, "You have seen me on the path of life. Now I am on the path of death." As he spoke, lines from his poem "Life Infinite" flashed through my mind:

Beyond words, this no-thingness within,
Which I've become. So to remain

Only one thing's needed: Zen sitting.
I think, breathe with my whole body—

Marvelous. The joy's so pure,
It's beyond lovemaking, anything.

I can see, live anywhere, everywhere.
I need nothing, not even life.

Shinkichi Takahashi was a remarkable poet. Few in our time have encompassed so much, left such a bracing legacy. How he achieved so much will, I am confident, engage the minds and talents of future scholars, but this I will claim for him: he found early in life what his life most needed, lived it, and wrote it as no other could.

The poet died the night of June 4, 1987. I could only lift my head with gratitude for having known him, and I now offer to his memory a few words:

June 5, 1987
While I wash dishes to
Gregorian chants, what
started out a ho-hum
day—the usual round

of doodles, chores,
anxieties—explodes
with a bright swallowtail
joyriding by the window,

looping where by whitest
columbines a robin, head
cocked to love sounds,
watches as a squirrel

near the old pear tree
quivers astride his mate.
The phone rings, bringing
word Shinkichi Takahashi

died last night.
                  And so
the world goes on. Now
the squirrels scamper

through the branches,
making leaves dance
like the poet's sparrows
wing-stroking an elegy in air.

LUCIEN STRYK